ELEMENTARY ENGLISH READING & WRITING

英文法から学ぶ英作と読解

佐藤 哲三

伊藤 真紀

NAN'UN-DO

Elementary English Reading & Writing

Copyright © 2015

Tetsuzo Sato
Maki Ito

All rights Reserved

*No part of this book may be reproduced in any form without written permission
from the authors and Nan'un-do Co., Ltd.*

このテキストの音声を無料で視聴（ストリーミング）・ダウンロードできます。自習用音声としてご活用ください。
以下のサイトにアクセスしてテキスト番号で検索してください。

https://nanun-do.com テキスト番号 [511663]

※ 無線 LAN（WiFi）に接続してのご利用を推奨いたします。

※ 音声ダウンロードは Zip ファイルでの提供になります。
お使いの機器によっては別途ソフトウェア（アプリケーション）の導入が必要となります。

※ Elementary English Reading & Writing の音声ダウンロードページは以下の QR コードからもご利用になれます。

はじめに

　本書は，まず一般に敬遠・軽視されがちな英文法事項をしっかりと復習し，次に事項確認の基礎英作と興味深い内容を含んだ応用英作をした後，英文読解に入れるように効率的に編まれた英作と読解の教材です。

　高校を卒業して大学等に入学するまでに英語を6年以上も学んで来たのに，自信を持って英語を読んだり，書いたり，話したり，聴いたりすることができないと思う人が意外に多いのではないでしょうか。その大きな原因のひとつに英文法力不足を挙げることができるでしょう。英語に限らず，一般に外国語をある一定の期間で習得しようと思えば，発音や語彙の学習は勿論のこと，十分な文法学習が必要となります。中学，高校の6年間を振り返ってみてください。英文法を身に付ける時間は十分でしたか。学年が進行するにつれて英語嫌い，英文法嫌いが増えることから，不十分だったのではないかと思われます。この点を解決しなければこの先も思うように英語力が身につかないでしょう。「急がば回れ」です。まず，英文法の効率的な再学習を大学等での英語学習の出発点にして，会話力，聴解力，読解力，英作力の向上に繋げて下さい。

　本書の各章は6頁立てで，構成は次のとおりです。まず「英文法」ですが，最初の頁がその章の文法事項の整理，2頁目がその文法事項の練習，次に「英作」ですが，3頁目と4頁目に単語の書き取り・並べ替え・和文英訳・応用英作が順に配列されています。最後に「英文読解」で5頁目が英文読解Ⅰ，6頁目が英文読解Ⅱになっています。「応用英作」と「英文読解Ⅱ」を除いては実用英語技能検定の3級・準2級レベルを想定して編まれています。そして，「英作」の単語の書き取り40問テストは基本語彙ながらも意外に綴れないでしょうから語頭文字と文字数をヒントに挑戦して下さい。「英文読解」の英文は必ずしもその章で学習する文法事項に十分に合致しているとは限りませんが，英検二次対策や速読にも利用できる内容になっています。

　今後，世界語としての英語を駆使して，自身の様々な情報を発信したり，意見を述べたりすることは，ますます不可欠なこととなってくるでしょう。そこで，これまでに英語がそれほど得意でなかった人，英語が嫌いではないにもかかわらず伸び悩んでいる人，そういった人たちが，本書を使うことで，発信型の英語の礎を築き上げていかれることを切に願っています。

　最後に，本書の出版を快諾された南雲堂の南雲一範社長，編集実務の行き届いたご配慮をいただいた加藤敦氏に心より感謝申し上げます。

2014年 秋

著者一同

CONTENTS

はしがき ... 3

Chapter 1 ５つの基本文型 ... 6
Five Basic Sentence Patterns

Chapter 2 動詞 ... 12
Verbs

Chapter 3 進行形・未来形・助動詞 ... 18
Progressive / Future / Auxiliary

Chapter 4 名詞・冠詞・代名詞 ... 24
Nouns / Articles / Pronouns

Chapter 5 前置詞・接続詞 (I) ... 30
Prepositions / Conjunctions (I)

Chapter 6 形容詞・副詞と比較級 ... 36
Adjectives / Adverbs / Comparison

Chapter 7 命令文・感嘆文 ... 42
Imperative and Exclamatory Sentences

Chapter 8	不定詞		48
	Infinitive		
Chapter 9	動名詞と分詞		54
	Gerund / Participle		
Chapter 10	各種疑問文・It の特別用法		60
	Interrogative / Usage of 'It'		
Chapter 11	受動態		66
	Passive		
Chapter 12	完了形		72
	Perfect		
Chapter 13	接続詞（II）（時制の一致を含む）		78
	Conjunctions (II) including Sequence of Tenses		
Chapter 14	仮定法		84
	Subjunctive		
Chapter 15	関係詞		90
	Relative		

Chapter 1　5つの基本文型

Grammar Check　02

1 ▶ 第1文型…主語(S)＋完全自動詞(V)

1) **Birds sing**.
2) The **sun sets** in the west.
3) Several **boys run** too slowly around the lake.
4) **Julia chatted** with her friend over coffee.
5) There **is** a **dog** at the door.

2 ▶ 第2文型…主語(S)＋不完全自動詞(V)＋主格補語(SC)

6) **He is** a **surgeon**.
7) **She is busy** every day.
8) **Alice looks happy**.
9) **She feels better** now than this morning.
10) The **leaves** have **turned red** in the mountains.

3 ▶ 第3文型…主語(S)＋完全他動詞(V)＋目的語(O)

11) **I like dogs**.
12) **They play football** every day.
13) **They enjoyed riding horses**.
14) **Rachel** often **loses** her **key**.
15) **They stopped talking** when the teacher came in.

4 ▶ 第4文型…主語(S)＋完全他動詞(V)＋間接目的語(IO)＋直接目的語(DO)

16) My **uncle gave me** a **camera**. = My uncle gave a camera **to** me.
17) **I wrote him** a long **letter**. = I wrote a long letter **to** him.
18) **He bought me** this **bike**. = He bought this bike **for** me.
19) **She cooked him meals**. = She cooked meals **for** him.
20) **They asked her** some **questions**. = They asked some questions **of** her.

5 ▶ 第5文型…主語(S)＋不完全他動詞(V)＋目的語(O)＋目的格補語(OC)

21) **We call him Ken**.
22) **He named** his **son Taro**.
23) **They made her happy**.
24) **I found** this **book** very **interesting**.

Exercises

A ▶ 次の英文の文型を答えなさい。

1. He was a student at this school.　　　　第(　　)文型
2. I will stay with my aunt.　　　　　　　　第(　　)文型
3. Keep your eyes closed.　　　　　　　　　第(　　)文型
4. I made Shun a new doghouse.　　　　　　第(　　)文型
5. I quite forgot her birthday.　　　　　　　第(　　)文型

B ▶ 次の英文の下線部が目的語か補語かを答えなさい。

1. Rachel is playing the <u>piano</u>.　　　　　　　(　　　　)
2. She will be a <u>star player</u> in the future.　　(　　　　)
3. His brother got <u>angry</u> over trifles.　　　　(　　　　)
4. My uncle told me an interesting <u>story</u>.　　(　　　　)
5. They made me <u>happy</u>.　　　　　　　　　(　　　　)

C ▶ 次の英文の下線部の語を文末に移動させて書き換えなさい。

1. Ben offered <u>Alice</u> his help.　　_____
2. They asked <u>me</u> several questions.　_____
3. I'll soon get <u>you</u> a pillow.　_____
4. Jack will buy <u>Jill</u> a beautiful comb.　_____
5. Please lend <u>me</u> ten dollars.　_____

D ▶ 次の英文を日本文に直しなさい。

1. The football season has already begun.

2. Seeing is believing.

3. You must write a letter in English.

4. I found the book very interesting.

5. She made me a Christmas cake.

E ▶ 次の各組の英文が同じ意味になるように(　)内に適切な語を書き入れなさい。

1. He is a hard worker. = He (　　　　) (　　　　).
2. They lived happily. = They lived a (　　　　) (　　　　).
3. Why did you say so? = (　　　　) made you say so?
4. This bike belongs to me. = This bike is (　　　　).
5. She can speak English well. = She is a (　　　　) (　　　　) of English.

Composition

Vocabulary ▶ 語頭文字と文字数をヒントに綴りなさい。

01. 固定する f-(6)	02. 夜明け d-(4)	03. 収穫 h-(7)	04. 目覚める a-(5)
05. 熱心な e-(5)	06. 捜す s-(6)	07. 寛大な g-(8)	08. 誠実な s-(7)
09. 仕える s-(5)	10. じっと見る s-(5)	11. 罰する p-(6)	12. 脳 b-(5)
13. 病気 d-(7)	14. 説明する e-(7)	15. 神経 n-(5)	16. 薬 m-(8)
17. 紹介する i-(9)	18. 気候 c-(7)	19. 痛む a-(4)	20. 邪悪な w-(6)
21. 謙虚な m-(6)	22. 引き裂く t-(4)	23. 舌 t-(6)	24. 利己的な s-(7)
25. 撒き散らす s-(7)	26. 支える s-(7)	27. 食欲 a-(8)	28. 誕生 b-(5)
29. 家具 f-(9)	30. がらくた g-(7)	31. 落ち着く s-(6)	32. ぜいたく l-(6)
33. 不在の a-(6)	34. 生きて a-(5)	35. 年配の e-(7)	36. 裸の n-(5)
37. 疲れきった w-(5)	38. 奪う r-(3)	39. 後悔する r-(6)	40. ごみ l-(6)

Rearranging ▶ 次の日本文に合うように[ ]内の語に**語頭文字が示された語を加えて**並べ替えなさい。

01. それらの部屋はどれも南向きではない。
    [(f   ) / of / the / neither / south / rooms].

02. 信号が赤になった。
    [(t   ) / light / the / has / traffic / red].

03. 彼はその次の日に日本から中国に向かった。
    [(l   ) / Japan / the / he / for / next / China / day].

04. 冷蔵庫は魚や肉を新鮮に保ってくれる。
    [(k   ) / fish / the / and / fresh / refrigerator / meat].

05. 父はよく私たちに興味深い話をしてくれた。
    [(t   ) / often / to / my / stories / father / us / interesting].

Basic Composition ▶ (　　)内の条件をヒントに英文に直しなさい。

01. 昨夜，Tom は Jane と踊った。　　　　　　　　　　　　　　　(6 語で)

02. 空には雲ひとつなかった。　　　　　　　　　　　　　　　　　(a を用いて 8 語で)

03. その結果はがっかりさせるようなものであった。　　　　　　　(the, was を用いて 4 語で)

04. 彼女のお兄さんは年の割には若く見える。　　　　　　　　　　(7 語で)

05. あなたは彼が私たちに言いたかったことがわかりましたか。　　(9 語で)

06. 一昨日，私は岩手にいる伯父に手紙を書いた。　　　　　　　　(13 語で)

07. コンピューターは私たちの手間を大いに省いてくれる。　　　　(save, work を用いて 8 語で)

08. 彼が私に魚の釣り方を教えてくれた。　　　　　　　　　　　　(7 語で)

09. その知らせを聞いて彼らは喜んだ。　　　　　　　　　　　　　(5 語で)

10. 彼女は車をよく整備（in good condition）している。　　　　　(7 語で)

Applied Composition ▶ 次の日本文に合うように，下の語(句)を並べ替えて正しい英文に直しなさい。

昔々，ある所に，お爺さんとお婆さんがいました。ある日，お爺さんは山へ柴刈りに，お婆さんは川へ洗濯に行きました。お婆さんが川で洗濯をしていると，川上から大きな桃が，どんぶらこっこ，どんぶらこっこと流れてきました。お婆さんは，その桃を「どっこいしょ」と拾い上げると，大事に抱えて家に帰りました。

(a time / an old man / once upon / and his old wife / out in the countryside / there lived). (while the old man / one day, / in the mountains / was up / gathering firewood, / went to the river / to do her laundry / the old woman). (the clothes, / scrubbing / an enormous peach / as she was / she noticed / bobbling and / the river / tumbling down). (with some / she fished / difficulty, / out of the water, / the giant peach / carried it home / and she carefully / with her).

Reading Comprehension I

▶次の文章を読み，後の問いに答えなさい。　　　　　　　　　03

An American woman was interested in the Japanese daily commute. At first, she was impressed by the cleanliness and orderliness of public transportation in Japan. Many people notice that ① (the subways in other countries are unreliable and dirty.)
　She thought of a way to make use of the commuting time. When she looked around in the subway, ② (she found a variety of ways to kill time.) Some people were reading newspapers or novels, etc. Others were playing with their cell phones or video games. ③ (In Japan, many people sleep while sitting or standing up.) This is an uncommon scene in other countries. Some say they have never seen people sleeping on the train outside Japan. ④ (This unique Japanese sleeping habit gives foreigners an impression) that ⑤ (hard work may make many Japanese people tired.)

注　be impressed by ~ 〜に感心する

1 ▶ (　) ①〜⑤を日本文に直し，それぞれの下線部を S, V, O, C に分類しなさい。

① the subways in other countries are unreliable and dirty.

_____

　the subways: (　　)　　are: (　　)　　unreliable and dirty: (　　)

② she found a variety of ways to kill time.

_____

　she: (　　)　　found: (　　)　　a variety of ways: (　　)

③ In Japan, many people sleep while sitting or standing up.

_____

　many people: (　　)　　sleep: (　　)

④ This unique Japanese sleeping habit gives foreigners an impression

_____

　This unique Japanese sleeping habit: (　　)　　gives: (　　)
　foreigners: (　　)　　an impression: (　　)

⑤ hard work may make many Japanese people tired.

_____

　hard work: (　　)　　may make: (　　)
　many Japanese people: (　　)　　tired: (　　)

Reading Comprehension II

▶次の文章を読み，後の問いに答えなさい。　　　　　　　　　　　04

> The Rolling Stones are the longest performing English rock band ever. They were formed in London in 1962 and are still performing today. Some members have left the band and others have joined it, but this band has continued over five decades without once breaking up.
>
> The origin of The Rolling Stones' music is blues. Blues originated in African-American communities of the United States around the end of the 19th century. While discrimination against African-Americans continued, they were inspired by the style of African-American music. That was a revolutionary idea in the 1960's. The former leader Brian Jones named the band "The Rolling Stones," after blues artist Muddy Waters' tune "Rollin' Stone."
>
> Mick Jagger and Keith Richards, main members from the beginning, have been friends since they were kids. In 2003 Tony Blair, (the) then British prime minister and huge fan of Mick Jagger, recommended him to the queen, and then Mick Jagger received knighthood for services to music. There is a side story that Keith Richards got angry with Mick Jagger because of his reception of knighthood.

注　(the) then 当時の（人名の後に同格名詞群の一部として付いているので the は省略可）
　　receive knighthood for services to ~ ~への貢献に対してナイト爵位を授与される

1 ▶次の質問に英語で答えなさい。

(1) When were The Rolling Stones formed?

　　_____

(2) What is the origin of the band's music?

　　_____

(3) Since when have Mick Jagger and Keith Richards been friends?

　　_____

(4) When did Mick Jagger receive knighthood?

　　_____

(5) Why did Keith Richards get angry with Mick Jagger?

　　_____

Chapter 2　動詞

Grammar Check　　05

1 ▶ be 動詞

1) I **am** a medical clerk and he is a pharmacist.
2) I**'m not** busy now. He **isn't** busy, either.
3) How **are** you? I'm fine, thank you.
4) Where **were** you yesterday? I **was** in Fukuoka.
5) There **aren't** any children in the park.

2 ▶ 一般動詞（現在形）

6) I **don't like** dogs.
7) The earth **revolves** around the sun.
8) He **doesn't** usually **have** coffee at meals.
9) **Do** you **know** him very well? No, I **don't**.
10) **Does** Bob **belong** to the baseball club? No, he **doesn't**.
11) Who **cooks** breakfast every morning? Mother **does**. / I **do**.

　　※　状態動詞 … be, know, belong, like など
　　※　動作動詞 … jump, cross, put, run など

3 ▶ 一般動詞（過去形）

12) I **slept** well last night.
13) Ben **changed** from his dirty clothes into clean ones.
14) I **studied** Latin at school, but I never **did learn** it.「…全然身につかなかった」
15) Tom **didn't leave** for London yesterday.
16) **Did** the volcano Mt. Sakurajima **erupt** a few days ago? No, it **didn't**.

4 ▶ 自動詞・他動詞と群動詞

17) The library **opens** at nine.
18) Please **open** the door.
19) Ken is **lying** on his stomach.
20) She **laid** her baby on the bed.
21) When the curtain **rises**, everybody **raises** his or her head.
22) What time will he **arrive in** Tokyo? = What time will he **reach** Tokyo?
23) They **approached** the room without a sound.
24) We **discussed** the matter with the teacher.
25) This fruit **resembles** that one in shape, but not in taste.
26) He didn't **respect** you. = He didn't **look up to** you.
27) She **endured** a week of hard training. = She **put up with** a week of hard training.

Exercises

A ▶ 次の英文の( )内から適切な語(句)を選びなさい。

1. There (is / are / was / were) a lot of children here a few hours ago.
2. My father (isn't / don't / doesn't / hasn't) drive on Sundays.
3. When did the plane (take / takes / took / taking) off?
4. She (belongs / is belonging / has belonged) to the tennis club for two years.

B ▶ 次の各組の英文が同じ意味になるように( )内に適切な語を書き入れなさい。

1. How many seasons are there in a year?
   = How many seasons (　　　　　) a year (　　　　　)?
2. Jack is a fast swimmer. = Jack can (　　　　　) (　　　　　).
3. Sachiko is a good speaker of English.
   = Sachiko (　　　　　) English (　　　　　).
4. We (　　　　　) a lot of snow here in winter.
   = It (　　　　　) a lot here in winter.

C ▶ 次の日本文を( )内の語(句)に1語を加えて英文に直しなさい。

1. あの歌の出だしはどうでしたか。(begin / song / how / that)?

2. 電車はあとどのくらいで博多駅に着きますか。
   (due to / soon / the train / at / how / arrive / Hakata Station)?

3. その小包はどれくらいの重さですか。
   (the parcel / much / weigh / how)? = (heavy / the parcel / how)?

4. 日本ではふつう家に入る前に靴を脱ぎます。
   (before / people / their / their / homes / entering / shoes / off) in Japan.

D ▶ 次の英文の( )内から適切な語(句)を選びなさい。

1. The lawyer insists (in / of / on) the man's innocence.
2. Don't (enter / enter at / enter in) the room without knocking.
3. When did he (marry / marry to / marry with) her?
4. Smoke (rised / rose / raised) from the factory chimneys.
5. They won't agree (about / over / with) me on this point.
6. TOEFL stands (at / for / in) Test of English as a Foreign Language.
7. He consented (of / on / to) my plan.
8. I (attended / attended at / attended to) a funeral last Friday.
9. Who will look (after / at / for) your pet dog while you are on a trip?
10. I'll catch up (on / to / with) you soon.

Composition

Vocabulary ▶ 語頭文字と文字数をヒントに綴りなさい。

01. 板	b-(5)	02. 人の姿	f-(6)	03. 世界的な	g-(6)	04. 球, 天体	s-(6)
05. 重さ	w-(6)	06. 刺激的な	e-(8)	07. 認める	r-(9)	08. 尊敬する	r-(7)
09. 文化	c-(7)	10. 知識	k-(9)	11. 彫刻	s-(9)	12. 古代の	a-(7)
13. 即座の	i-(9)	14. 海峡	c-(7)	15. 地平線	h-(7)	16. 宇宙	u-(8)
17. 賞賛する	a-(6)	18. 喜ばせる	d-(7)	19. 驚く	w-(6)	20. 体育館	g-(9)
21. 記念碑	m-(8)	22. 光り輝く	b-(9)	23. 繊細な	d-(8)	24. 鋭い	k-(4)
25. 主唱者	a-(8)	26. 創造的な	c-(8)	27. 個人	i-(10)	28. 女性	f-(6)
29. 進歩	a-(7)	30. 滑らかな	s-(6)	31. 臆病者	c-(6)	32. 配達する	d-(7)
33. 伸ばす	e-(6)	34. 退く	r-(6)	35. 地区	d-(8)	36. 地方	p-(8)
37. 再び始める	r-(6)	38. のままである	r-(6)	39. 方向	d-(9)	40. 表面	s-(7)

Rearranging ▶ 次の日本文に合うように [ ] 内の語(句)に**語頭文字が示された語を加えて**並べ替えなさい。

01. 彼はクラスの他の学生に遅れないように努めている。
    [(k   ) / up / the other / the class / in / with / to / he / students / tries].

02. 私はバスが遅れるだろうと思っている。
    [(e   ) / to / late / I / bus / be / the].

03. 法の下では全ての人間は平等である。
    [(a   ) / humans / the / law / all / equal / under].

04. Tom は友人を訪ねたが, 家には誰もいなかった。
    [(c   ) / his friend, / Tom / home / was / at / on / there / but / nobody].

05. 彼女の行動はいつもながらの色々なうわさを生んだ。
    [(b   ) / rumors / forth / crop of / the usual / her action].

Basic Composition ▶ (　　)内の条件をヒントに英文に直しなさい。

01. 私はそのコートを安かったので買った。　　　　　(because, cheap を用いて 8 語で)

02. 私は 6 時の電車に間に合うように早く起きた。　　(the 6:00 train を用いて 9 語で)

03. 春にはたくさんの美しい花々が咲く。　　　　　　(bloom を用いて 6 語で)

04. はさみは下から 2 番目の引き出しの中にある。　　(drawer を用いて 10 語で)

05. なぜあなたは昨日学校に遅れたのですか。　　　　(late を用いて 7 語で)

06. 彼女が戻ってくるまでここで待ちましょう。　　　(until を用いて 7 語で)

07. あなたが手を貸してくれたのでとても手間が省けました。　(saved, lot を用いて 8 語で)

08. その提案に賛成ですか，それとも反対ですか。　　(for, proposal を用いて 7 語で)

09. 誕生日に何が欲しいですか。　　　　　　　　　　(for を用いて 7 語で)

10. 明日雨が降れば，家にいる。　　　　　　　　　　(stay at を用いて 9 語で)

Applied Composition ▶ 次の日本文に合うように，下の語(句)を並べ替えて正しい英文に直しなさい。

観光は産業革命以降に起こった最近の現象である。「ツーリズム（観光）」という言葉が英語に現れたのは 19 世紀初頭になってからのことである。そして「ツアー（旅行）」という言葉は，個人が旅行するよりは，劇団などのグループが巡業に出ることを連想させるものであった。

(*tourism* / that / the Industrial Revolution / is / after / a / recent phenomenon / developed). (in / until / the word *tourism* / did not / nineteenth century / appear / the English language / the early). (and the word *tour* / was more / of people, / closely associated with a journey or / a circuit by a group / such as / than / a theatrical company, / making a trip / of an individual / the idea / for pleasure purposes.)

Reading Comprehension I

▶次の文章を読み，後の問いに答えなさい。　06

　Animal-assisted therapy is a healing method using certified animals. This therapy ①(　　　　) regarded as an important part of treatment for a lot of people. These people ②(　　　　) physically, emotionally, or cognitively challenged. Animals such as rabbits, horses, cats and dolphins can (1) <u>make</u> good therapy animals, but dogs ③(　　　　) the most common.

　Regardless of the dog's breed, size, and age, any dog can (2) <u>graduate</u> as a therapy dog. But the dog needs several characteristics in order to become a therapy dog. The dog must ④(　　　　) friendly, non-aggressive, confident, calm, and receptive to training. A dog that (3) <u>barks</u> loudly at strangers is not suitable for a therapy dog. It ⑤(　　　　) often the case that therapy dogs have their own disabilities or have experienced abuse themselves.

　ⒶTrained dogs and handlers visit hospitals, nursing homes, or children's homes. The old people and children (4) <u>spend</u> a little time with therapy dogs, walking them and playing with them. ⒷThe therapy dogs can cheer up patients' minds and gradually help their recovery.

注　certified 資格のある　cognitively 認知の　abuse 虐待

1 ▶(　)①〜⑤の中に be 動詞を適切な形に直して書き入れなさい。

① (　　　　　)　② (　　　　　)　③ (　　　　　)
④ (　　　　　)　⑤ (　　　　　)

2 ▶下線 (1) 〜 (4) の一般動詞が自動詞か他動詞か答えなさい。

(1) (　　　　　)　　(2) (　　　　　)
(3) (　　　　　)　　(4) (　　　　　)

3 ▶下線部ⒶⒷを日本文に直しなさい。

Ⓐ　Trained dogs and handlers visit hospitals, nursing homes, or children's homes.

　_____

　_____

Ⓑ　The therapy dogs can cheer up patients' minds and gradually help their recovery.

　_____

　_____

Reading Comprehension II

▶次の文章を読み，後の問いに答えなさい。　　　　　　　　　　　　07

　Do you know about Western wedding traditions? One of the most famous traditions is the so-called "something four": "something old, something new, something borrowed, something blue … and a silver sixpence in her shoe." This comes from an old English song.

　"Something four" is a group of four good-luck charms for brides on their wedding day. First, "something old" symbolizes the link with the bride's own family, so brides usually wear their mother's or grandmother's jewellery. Second, "something new" stands for good luck and a bright future in the bride's new married life. Brides generally pick out and wear newly-purchased items such as accessories or gloves. Third, "something borrowed" means that friends and family will be there for the bride when help is needed, so they commonly lend her something like jewellery or a handkerchief from happy married friends. The fourth "something blue," such as a blue flower or accessory was a symbol of purity and trueness in the old days.

　A sixpence coin has been regarded as a lucky charm since the Victorian age. This charm is believed to bring brides wealth and prosperity. On the wedding day they wear a sixpence in their shoes.

1 ▶次の質問に英語で答えなさい。

(1) What is the "something four?"

　_____

(2) What does "something old" symbolize?

　_____

(3) Who do brides borrow some jewellery or a handkerchief from?

　_____

(4) What kind of symbol was "something blue" in the old days?

　_____

(5) What is believed to bring brides wealth and prosperity?

　_____

Chapter 3 進行形・未来形・助動詞

Grammar Check　　08

1 ▶ 現在・過去進行形…〈be 動詞＋現在分詞〉

   1)　He **is playing** tennis with her.
   2)　They **are not studying** but **watching** TV.
   3)　I **was washing** my car then.
   4)　**Are** you **working** now?—Yes, I **am**.

   ※　状態動詞は、原則として進行形にしない。

2 ▶ 未来形…単純未来，意志未来

   5)　I **shall be** twenty years old next year.
   6)　It **will rain** this afternoon.
   7)　She **will visit** us next month.
   8)　I **am going to sell** this car.

3 ▶ can, must, may, will, shall, should, need, dare, ought to

   9)　She **can** make sandwiches.
   10)　**Can** I use your bicycle?
   11)　**Can** the news be true?
   12)　The news **cannot** be true.
   13)　You **must** work harder than before.
   14)　He **must** be our teacher.
   15)　**May** I come in?—Yes, you may. / Yes, please do.
   16)　It **may** snow tonight.
   17)　**May** you live long!
   18)　**Will** you open the window?—**All right**.
   19)　**Shall I** turn on the radio?—Yes, please.
   20)　**Shall we** go to the movies?—Yes, let's.
   21)　You **should** come earlier.
   22)　You **shouldn't** go out so late at night.
   23)　You **need not** buy that book.
   24)　**Need** I go now?
   25)　I **dared not** tell her the sad news.　「あえて〜しなかった」
   26)　**How dare** you say such a thing?　「よくもまあ〜できるものだ」
   27)　You **oughtn't to** say such a thing.
   28)　That **ought to** be an exciting game.

Exercises

A ▶ 次の英文の( )内から適切な語(句)を選びなさい。

1. He (used to / should) go to school by bus, but now he goes by subway.
2. You (mustn't / needn't) make your bed. I will do it.
3. There (would / used to) be a clean stream here.
4. You (ought / should) not to eat so much.
5. (Would / Should) you mind lending me some money?

B ▶ 次の各組の英文が同じ意味になるように( )内に適切な語を書き入れなさい。

1. Don't throw stones at the dog.
   You (　　　　　　) throw stones at the dog.
2. Dick wasn't able to go on a picnic yesterday.
   Dick (　　　　　　) go on a picnic yesterday.
3. It is not necessary for you to pay the money.
   You (　　　　　　) pay the money.
4. It is impossible for me to write the report in a day.
   I (　　　　　　) write the report in a day.
5. Surely she missed the 8:20 train.
   She (　　　　　　) have missed the 8:20 train.

C ▶ 次の英文を日本文に直しなさい。

1. I will do my best to the last.
   _____
2. The sun is about to sink below the horizon.
   _____
3. Can the rumor be true?—No, it can't be.
   _____

D ▶ 次の日本文を英文に直しなさい。

1. 私がLondonに着いたとき，雨が降っていた。
   _____
2. Andrewは間違えてばかりいる。　　　　　（進行形で）
   _____
3. 私は自分の自動車を売ることにしている。（goingを用いて）
   _____
4. 今夜天気はどうなりますか。　　　　（WhatとHowを用いて2通りで）
   _____
   _____
5. 宿題を手伝ってもらえませんか。　　　　　（willを用いて）
   _____

Composition

Vocabulary ▶ 語頭文字と文字数をヒントに綴りなさい。

01. 活動的な a-(6)	02. 真剣な e-(7)	03. 雇う e-(6)	04. 反対する o-(6)
05. 品質 q-(7)	06. 量 q-(8)	07. 人工の a-(10)	08. 自信のある c-(9)
09. 巨大な h-(4)	10. 客観的な o-(9)	11. 表現する e-(7)	12. 険しい s-(5)
13. 吠える r-(4)	14. 幅広い b-(5)	15. ごく小さい t-(4)	16. 敵の h-(7)
17. 中空の h-(6)	18. 原理 p-(9)	19. 目的 p-(7)	20. 拒絶する r-(6)
21. 予定 s-(8)	22. 建設する c-(9)	23. 像 i-(5)	24. 改良する i-(7)
25. 不平を言う c-(8)	26. 獲得する o-(6)	27. 香り s-(5)	28. 悲鳴 s-(6)
29. つかむ s-(5)	30. 管理する m-(6)	31. 禁ずる f-(6)	32. 成功する s-(7)
33. (人,罪などを)許す f-(7)	34. 解く s-(5)	35. 許す p-(6)	36. 発明 i-(9)
37. 望ましい d-(9)	38. 主張する i-(6)	39. 手続き p-(9)	40. 認める a-(5)

Rearranging ▶ 次の日本文に合うように [ ] 内の語に**語頭文字が示された語を加えて**並べ替えなさい。

01. 私たちは軽井沢で楽しんでいる。
    [(h   ) / a / at / we / Karuizawa / time / good / are].

02. 隣の犬はいつも吠えてばかりいる。
    [(b   ) / all / dog / the / my / is / neighbor's / time].

03. 彼女が電話をかけてきたとき,私は入浴中だった。
    [(t   ) / called / I / me / she / when / a / was / bath].

04. 彼女はいつも他人のあら捜しばかりしていた。
    [(f   ) / always / others / fault / was / with / she].

05. 明朝はまだ雪が降っているだろう。
    [(b   ) / will / morning / it / still / snowing / tomorrow].

Basic Composition ▶ (　)内の条件をヒントに英文に直しなさい。

01. Tom は先週からずっと Jane に会えずにいる。　　　(able, see を用いて 11 語で)

02. 彼の身に何か起こったのかもしれない。　　　(happen を用いて 6 語で)

03. あなた方お二人の幸せを祈ります。　　　(may を用いて 5 語で)

04. あなたは次の日曜日には出社しなければならないだろう。　　　(9 語で)

05. 昨夜は激しく雨が降ったに違いない。　　　(7 語で)

06. 私は子供のころよくその湖につりに行ったものだ。　　　(would を用いて 11 語で)

07. あなたはその映画を見ればよかったのに。　　　(should を用いて 6 語で)

08. 彼が怒るのは当然だ。　　　(natural, should を用いて 8 語で)

09. 兄は正午までにはここに着くはずだ。　　　(ought を用いて 8 語で)

Applied Composition ▶ 次の日本文に合うように，下の語(句)を並べ替えて正しい英文に直しなさい。

人間の先祖が草食動物であった遠い昔では，盲腸は現代人のそれよりもっと重要な役割を果たしていた。人間は雑食なので，主に消化の良い食物を食べるようになり，盲腸に送られる消化しきれない食物は少なくなっている。その結果，盲腸は余分なものとなり，仕事を失ったような状態である。それゆえ，盲腸はまさに付加物であり，「余分なもの」や「付属品」の代名詞であると言われるのである。

(long, long ago / were herbivorous, / when / in digestion / our ancestors / the appendix played / that of / a more active part / than / human beings today). (since humans / and primarily eat / are omnivorous, / is passed / digestible food, / into the appendix / less undigested food). (redundant, / the appendix / as a result, / as if / has become / it were unemployed). (people / or an *attachment* / the appendix is /, therefore, / really an appendix / say that / —a synonym / for *something extra*).

Reading Comprehension I

▶次の文章を読み，後の問いに答えなさい。　09

Advanced technology ⓐ (overwhelms) our daily lives. Cellphones and computers have been crucial to our lives in recent decades. Now the handy portable computer known as the smartphone has become a best friend for many people rather than just a material object. Regardless of age, gender, nationality, ethnicity, career, or economic status, ① quite a few people are always carrying a smartphone. The smartphone market will continue to grow steadily all over the world.

② It must be convenient to have a smartphone, but the number of smartphone addicts is growing. Smartphone addiction is becoming a social problem throughout the world. Many researchers point out that smartphone addiction [   ] affect development in teenagers. It could lead to conditions such as sleep disorders, autonomic imbalance, or depression.

注　crucial 不可欠な　ethnicity 民族性　addict 中毒者　autonomic imbalance 自律神経失調症　depression うつ病

1 ▶ ⓐの（　）内の語を進行形に直しなさい。

(　　　　　　　　　　)

2 ▶ [　]内に適切な助動詞を下の語群から選びなさい。

[　　　　　　]

| ought to | need | cannot | may |

3 ▶ 下線部①②を日本文に直しなさい。

① quite a few people are always carrying a smartphone

② It must be convenient to have a smartphone

Reading Comprehension II

▶次の文章を読み，後の問いに答えなさい。

Would you like a cup of tea? "Afternoon tea" is the British custom of taking a break to drink tea with sweets at a certain time during the day. It is believed that the custom began in the early 19th century. In those days, the English had two main meals a day: breakfast and dinner. However, dinner time was usually between 8 and 9 p.m. When the Duchess of Bedford was suffering from hunger and a "sinking feeling" by late afternoon, she requested some food and drink: "Will you bring tea, bread and butter, and cakes for me?" Later, she made a habit of inviting her friends to enjoy a light "tea time" in the afternoon at home. This custom gradually spread throughout England. Now afternoon tea has become popular with foreign tourists.

For afternoon tea, we start with small cucumber sandwiches, and next eat scones with jam and clotted cream, and finally have some cakes served on the top of a three-tiered cake stand. Eating all this may be too much, and you certainly don't need to finish. But the important thing is that you enjoy the graceful and traditional atmosphere of British afternoon tea.

注　the Duchess of Bedford ベッドフォード公爵夫人　sinking feeling 虚脱感
clotted cream 凝固させた濃厚クリーム　three-tiered 3段の

1 ▶次の質問に英語で答えなさい。

(1) When did the custom of afternoon tea begin?

_____

(2) How many meals a day did the English have?

_____

(3) Did the Duchess of Bedford always enjoy the light "tea time" by herself?

_____

(4) Who is afternoon tea popular with?

_____

(5) For afternoon tea, what do we start with?

_____

Chapter 4　名詞・冠詞・代名詞

Grammar Check　🔵 11

1 ▶ 普通名詞・集合名詞・物質名詞・抽象名詞・固有名詞

1) I am a **student**, and they are **students** too.
2)-1 My **family is** very large.（集合体として）
2)-2 My **family are all** early risers.（構成員に着目）
2)-3 There **are** ten **families** in the apartment building.
3) Please give me **a glass of water**.
4) **Honesty** is the best policy.
5)-1 **Abraham Lincoln** was the 16th president of **the United States**.
5)-2 **The Tanakas** like dogs better than cats.

2 ▶ 不定冠詞・定冠詞・冠詞の省略

6)-1 She waited for **an** hour.
6)-2 **A cat** can see in the dark.（総称的）
　　= **The cat** can see in the dark. = **Cats** can see in the dark.
7)-1 There is a book there. **The** book is written in English.（前述の名詞の指示）
7)-2 **The** earth moves around **the** sun.（唯一のもの）
7)-3 He likes playing **the flute**.（楽器名）
8)-1 I have **breakfast** at seven.（食事名）
　　cf. She had **a nice dinner** yesterday.（修飾語付き）
8)-2 We walked to **school**.（授業）cf. We walked to **the school**.（建物）

3 ▶ 人称代名詞・所有代名詞・再帰代名詞・疑問代名詞・指示代名詞・不定代名詞

9) Do **you** know **her** sister?
10)-1 Is that house **yours** or **theirs**?
10)-2 She is a friend of **mine**.
11)-1 I enjoyed **myself** at the party.（再帰用法）
11)-2 He **himself** did it.（同格的に用いて強調する）
11)-3 She made the bookcase **by herself**.（慣用句）
12)-1 **Which** do you like better, this or that?
12)-2 **What** do you call your dog?
12)-3 I don't know **who she is**.（間接疑問）
13) Are **these** my children? Cf. Are **those** cats yours?（指示形容詞）
14)-1 **All** of the students **are** absent. cf. **All is** well with her.
14)-2 I have two sons. **One** is in Fukuoka, and **the other** is in Kyoto.
14)-3 He didn't say **anything**.
14)-4 **Each** of the students has a car.

Exercises

A ▶ 次の英文の下線部に（　）内の語を正しい形に直して書き入れなさい。

1. Mr. White is six _____ three _____ tall.　(foot, inch)
2. How many _____ does this apartment building hold?　(family)
3. Our grandfather told us a lot of interesting _____ .　(story)
4. I have five _____ and seven _____ .　(nephew, niece)

B ▶ 次の英文の（　）内に下の語群から適切な語を選び正しい形に直して書き入れなさい。

1. My brother drank two (　　　　) of hot coffee this morning.
2. Bring me a (　　　　) of red chalk, please.
3. Please put a (　　　　) of sugar in my tea.
4. I bought two (　　　　) of bread yesterday.

glass	cup	loaf	piece	lump

C ▶ 次の英文の（　）内に適切な冠詞を書き入れなさい。不要な箇所には×印をつけなさい。

1. I have (　　　) dinner in (　　　) evening.
2. He told the helper to close (　　　) window.
3. He plays (　　　) tennis and she plays (　　　) violin after school.
4. By (　　　) way, who opened (　　　) drawers?

D ▶ 次の英文の（　）内から適切な語(句)を選びなさい。

1. I don't want this motorcycle. Do you want (it / one)?
2. Do you know (that / those) girls?
3. "(Who / Whose) is this book?" "It's my brother's."
4. He said to (his / himself), "What's the matter with her?"
5. I have two pens. One is long and (another / the other) is short.
6. (Each / Every) of the girls has her own camera.
7. (What / Which) of the books do you want to take?
8. "(Who / What) is she?" "She is a nurse."
9. (Either / Both) you or I must go there.

E ▶ 次の英文の下線部に（　）内の語を正しい形に直して書き入れなさい。

1. She visited _____ the day before yesterday.　(he)
2. Is that bicycle _____ or his?　(she)
3. Both of _____ are dead.　(they)
4. Do you know _____ bicycle that is?　(who)
5. I bowed to him and seated _____ .　(I)

Composition

Vocabulary ▶ 語頭文字と文字数をヒントに綴りなさい。

01. 争い　　　c-(8)　　02. 産する　　y-(5)　　03. 徐々の　　g-(7)　　04. 説明する　a-(7)

05. 出発　　　d-(9)　　06. 類推　　　a-(7)　　07. 感覚　　　s-(5)　　08. 誤った　　w-(5)

09. いたずら　m-(8)　　10. 残酷な　　c-(5)　　11. 見込み　　p-(8)　　12. 悩ます　　b-(6)

13. おどし　　t-(6)　　14. 必要な　　n-(9)　　15. 裁判する　j-(5)　　16. みなす　　r-(6)

17. ため息　　s-(4)　　18. 湿り気のある m-(5)　19. 意見　　　o-(7)　　20. 生命の　　v-(5)

21. 選挙する　e-(5)　　22. 粘り強い　t-(5)　　23. 内容　　　c-(7)　　24. 現れる　　a-(6)

25. 外国で　　a-(6)　　26. 格安品　　b-(7)　　27. 図案　　　d-(6)　　28. 発達する　d-(7)

29. 続く　　　c-(8)　　30. 起こる　　o-(5)　　31. 特性　　　p-(8)　　32. 繰り返す　r-(6)

33. 手がかり　c-(4)　　34. 完全にする c-(8)　　35. 倹約　　　t-(6)　　36. 要因　　　f-(6)

37. 階上に　　u-(8)　　38. 大部分　　m-(6)　　39. 創立する　e-(9)　　40. 増す　　　i-(8)

Rearranging ▶ 次の日本文に合うように［　］内の語に**語頭文字が示された語を加えて**並べ替えなさい。

01. 私の部屋には家具はあまりない。
    [(m　　　　) / furniture / room / I / my / don't / in / have].

02. 彼の農場にはたくさんの牛と羊がいる。
    [(s　　　　) / lots / on / of / he / his / has / cows / farm / and].

03. それは最初から最後まで興味深い本だ。
    [(e　　　　) / was / novel / it / from / to / interesting / beginning / an].

04. 私たちはそのボートを時間決め（1時間いくら）で借りた。
    [(t　　　　) / by / the / we / hour / hired / boat].

05. 成功は勤勉な人たちのところにやって来るものだ。
    [(t　　　　) / are / come / success / who / diligent / to / will].

06. 天は自ら助くる者を助く。
　　[(t　　　　　　) / those / helps / help / who / heaven].
　　_____

07. 日本の人口はフランスのおよそ2倍である。
　　[(t　　　　　　) / of / of / Japan / France / the / twice / population / is / about].
　　_____

Basic Composition ▶ （　）内の条件をヒントに英文に直しなさい。

01. 私のクラスの者は全員，今朝，出席している。　　（classmates を用いて7語で）

02. この薬を1日に3回服用しなさい。　　（7語で）

03. 地球は月よりはるかに大きい。　　（far bigger を用いて8語で）

04. この硬貨は銀でできている。　　（6語で）

05. 窓に鍵をかけないでおいたのは私だ。　　（it, left, unlocked を用いて8語で）

06. 陰で他人の悪口を言うべきではない。　　（ill, behind, back を用いて10語で）

07. 鶏肉の好きな人もいれば，好きでない人もいる。　　（some を用いて7語で）

Applied Composition ▶ 次の日本文に合うように，下の語(句)を並べ替えて正しい英文に直しなさい。

盲導犬を連れている人を街で見かけることがあります。これは目の不自由な人のための犬で，アメリカでは一般に seeing-eye dog と呼ばれていて，日本でも一般的になってきています。では，耳の不自由な人のための犬はどうでしょうか。アメリカでは，多くの耳の不自由な人も聴導犬を所有しているのを知っていましたか。

(come across / we / with a guide dog / sometimes / a person / on the street). (to lead him / a person / is / blind / most likely / and / is specially / the dog / such / trained). ("seeing-eye dogs" / guide dogs / called / are generally / in the United States). (in Japan as well / they / popular / have become / to some degree). (but / the deaf / guide dogs / what about / for)? (own / did you know / such guide dogs / many deaf people / that / in America / , too)?

Reading Comprehension I

▶次の文章を読み，後の問いに答えなさい。　　　　　　　　　　　　12

The International Space Station (ISS) is the greatest joint scientific program in the history of mankind. The United States, through NASA, chiefly organizes the ISS project, and < it / are / countries / 14 / in / other / participating >, such as Russia, Canada, France, and Japan. The ISS is a huge facility to observe space and the Earth and to conduct research and a variety of experiments in the cosmic environment. ① Each of the participating countries combines significant technology. The construction of the space station began in Earth's orbit in 1998 and was completed in July of 2011. ② The ISS can orbit the Earth 16 times a day.

Japan built the experiment module called "KIBO" on the ISS. Japanese astronaut Koichi Wakata used his great skill with the robot arm to contribute to the construction, and he became the first Japanese commander of the ISS in 2014. He thought that having dinner together with other crew members was important for a sense of unity. Wakata will continue to collect ⓐ (　　　　) information from ⓑ (　　　　) experiments in the future.

注　　facility 施設　　combine ～を集める　　orbit 軌道・軌道の周りを回る
　　　astronaut 宇宙飛行士　　contribute to ~ ～に貢献する　　commander 船長

1 ▶＜　＞内の語を「14の他の国々がそれに参加している」という意味になるように並べ替えなさい。

< it / are / countries / 14 / in / other / participating >

_____

2 ▶（　）ⓐⓑにそれぞれ「多くの」という意味を表す適切な語を書き入れなさい。

ⓐ　(　　　　　　　　) information

ⓑ　(　　　　　　　　) experiments

3 ▶下線部①②を日本文に直しなさい。

① Each of the participating countries combine significant technology.

_____

_____

② The ISS can orbit the Earth 16 times a day.

_____

_____

Reading Comprehension II

▶次の文章を読み，後の問いに答えなさい。

Sloths are mammals that live in the tropical rain forests of South America. They are leaf eaters. They sometimes also eat insects and small lizards.

Sloths have several unique features. They move very slowly and sleep more than 16 hours a day. They usually stay in the same tree their whole lives. But the female sloths move to a different tree after childbirth. They have very long claws to move up trees easier and avoid falling to the ground. Their long, curved claws allow them to hang upside down from branches easily, so they usually sleep and even give birth hanging from branches. Thanks to their flexible necks, they can turn their heads up to 270 degrees and see their surroundings without moving very much. Surprisingly, they can also swim very well.

Their meals are only 8 grams a day, so they must conserve their energy. The key is controlling their temperature. During the day their body temperature is from 30 to 34 degrees Celsius, but at night it falls to 25 degrees.

How can they protect against the danger of predators? Sloth fur is the color of the trees, so their bodies appear to be branches. For another thing, their movement is so slow that predators that have dynamic vision cannot catch sight of the sloths. It seems that laziness may be of great help to survival.

注　conserve ~ ～が失われないよう大切に使う　predators 肉食動物
　　dynamic vision 動体視力　laziness 怠ける事

1 ▶次の質問に英語で答えなさい。

(1) Where do sloths live?

(2) What do sloths eat?

(3) Why can sloths hang upside down from branches easily?

(4) How can sloths control their energy despite eating small meals?

(5) What does sloth fur look like?

Chapter 5　前置詞・接続詞 (I)

Grammar Check　　14

1 ▶ 前置詞

   1) School begins **at** nine and it is over **at** four.（時の一点）
   2) Turn right **at** the next corner.（場所の一点）
   3) We have to finish the work **by** tomorrow.（期限）
   4) I went from Fukuoka to Sapporo **by** plane.（交通手段）
   5) He wants to work **for** world peace.（目的・追求）
   6) It has been raining **for** more than five hours.（期間）
   7) How far is it **from** here to your school?（起点）
   8) Where do you come **from**?（出身）
   9) Tom lives **in** Kyoto.（場所・位置）
  10) I will be back **in** an hour.（経過時間）
  11) I am a member **of** the tennis club.（所属）
  12) This desk is made **of** wood.（材料）
  13) There is a world map **on** the wall.（接触）
  14) My father is at home **on** Sunday.（日・日付）
  15) She went **to** France last year.（到達点）
  16) We should be kind **to** old people.（関係）
  17) I usually go to school **with** Akio.（同伴）
  18) I have a meal **with** chopsticks.（道具）
  19) They went **out of** the room.（外向運動）
  20) She ran **into** the classroom.（内向運動）
  21) I waited for her **till** (**until**) seven o'clock.（継続）
  22) There are five bridges **over** the river.（真上）
  23) The cat **under** the tree is Lucy's.（真下）
  24) We remained in the bomb shelter **during** the air raid.（特定の期間中）

2 ▶ 等位接続詞（See Ch. 13),「時」,「条件」,「原因・理由」を表す従属接続詞（See Ch. 13）

  25) Both Jack **and** Jill went to the movies yesterday.
  26) He is old, **but** he is still strong.
  27) Go straight ahead, **and** you will see the post office on your left.
  28) Hurry up, **or** you will miss the train.
  29) **When** he arrives home, we'll go out for dinner.
  30) **If** it rains tomorrow, I won't go out.
     * 時，条件を表す副詞節では，未来のことでも現在形で表す。
  31) She scolded him, **because** he told a lie.

Exercises

A ▶ 次の英文の( )内から適切な語を選びなさい。

1. There is a big mosquito (of / on / over) the wall.
2. Several strangers are standing (at / above / between) the gate.
3. What are you wearing (in / at / under) your coat?
4. That is a limited express bus (on / by / for) Fukuoka.
5. We chatted about the soccer game (in / on / over) coffee.

B ▶ 次の英文の( )内に適切な前置詞を書き入れなさい。

1. Tires are made (   ) rubber.
2. Taro was born (   ) the morning of January 1.
3. He was staying (   ) a hotel (   ) Chicago.
4. I met her there (   ) chance.
5. She bought a doll (   ) twenty dollars.

C ▶ 次の英文を日本文に直しなさい。

1. The crops are dying for want of rain.

2. Admission is free for children below the age of five.

3. In case of fire, press this button.

4. That man saved his son from drowning at the cost of his life.

5. He went out in spite of the bad weather.

D ▶ 次の英文の( )内に下の語群から適切な語を選び書き入れなさい。

1. (   ) he opened the door, the students stopped chatting at once.
2. (   ) the weather is fine tomorrow, we will have a barbecue in the garden.
3. He is not a teacher, (   ) a scholar.
4. I was late (   ) the car broke down.
5. Hurry up, (   ) you can catch the 7:30 am express bus.
6. I'll make you lunch (   ) I finish cleaning.
7. Wear a warm sweater, (   ) you will catch cold.
8. It is true that she is young, (   ) she is well experienced.

| and | but | or | if | because | when | after |

Composition

Vocabulary ▶ 語頭文字と文字数をヒントに綴りなさい。

01. 賛成する　a-(7)　　02. 相続人　h-(4)　　03. 同意　a-(6)　　04. 征服する　c-(7)

05. 粗い　c-(6)　　06. 上昇　a-(6)　　07. 小麦粉　f-(5)　　08. 原子核　n-(7)

09. 組織する　o-(8)　　10. 恩義　o-(10)　　11. 岸壁　q-(4)　　12. 源　s-(6)

13. 場面　s-(5)　　14. 電気　e-(11)　　15. 原料　m-(8)　　16. 代用品　s-(10)

17. 同意する　c-(7)　　18. 許す　g-(5)　　19. 占領する　o-(6)　　20. 結果　c-(11)

21. 風変わりな　e-(9)　　22. 優秀な　e-(9)　　23. 死ぬ　p-(6)　　24. 貴重な　p-(8)

25. 適当な　p-(6)　　26. 減らす　d-(8)　　27. もがく　s-(8)　　28. 証拠　e-(8)

29. 確信　c-(9)　　30. 見捨てる　a-(7)　　31. 維持する　m-(8)　　32. 考案する　c-(8)

33. 実験　e-(10)　　34. 幽霊　g-(5)　　35. うわさ　r-(5か6)　　36. 夢想　r-(7)

37. 達成する　a-(6)　　38. 魅力　a-(10)　　39. まさる　e-(6)　　40. 応用　a-(11)

Rearranging ▶ 次の日本文に合うように[　]内の語に**前置詞か接続詞を加えて**並べ替えなさい。

01. 私はその絵を壁に掛けるつもりだ。
    [（前置詞　　　）/ the / the / hang / will / I / wall / painting].

02. 彼は休暇の間ずっと10時間勉強した。
    [（前置詞　　　）/ he / ten / the / vacation / studied / for / hours].

03. 彼は福岡のホテルに滞在していた。
    [（前置詞　　　）/ in / hotel / a / Fukuoka / staying / he / was].

04. 彼らはその計画に賛成ですか，それとも反対ですか。
    [（前置詞　　　）/ or / against / the / they / plan / are]?

05. あなたか私のどちらかが会合に出席しなければならない。
    [（接続詞　　　）/ to / the / you / I / meeting / attend / either / have].

06. 雨が止むまであそこで待とう。
   [（接続詞　　　　　）/ there / the / over / let's / stops / wait / rain].

07. もし明日雨が降らなければ、ハイキングに行くだろう。
   [（接続詞　　　　　）/ will / rains / go / it / we / on / hike / a / tomorrow].

08. 貧しいからといって人を軽蔑してはいけない。
   [（接続詞　　　　　）/ he / you / despise / poor / a / not / man / is / must].

Basic Composition ▶ (　)内の条件をヒントに英文に直しなさい。

01. 私たちのほとんどが、何らかの時にジーンズをはく。　(at one time を用いて10語で)

02. 私の母は年の割には若く見える。　(look, for を用いて7語で)

03. この花を英語で何と呼びますか。　(you を用いて8語で)

04. 先々週、私は青森にいる叔母に手紙を書いた。　(last を用いて13語で)

05. 彼は突然立ち止まった、というのも目前に大きな熊が立ちはだかったからだ。　(there, stood, ahead を用いて12語で)

06. 春が来て、彼らは穀粒（grain）を蒔いた。　(6語で)

07. ココナツの木(the coconut tree)は根が(its roots)そこで楽に水を見つけ出す(find water there)ことができるので、海の近くに育つ。　(15語で)

Applied Composition ▶ 次の日本文に合うように、下の語(句)を並べ替えて正しい英文に直しなさい。

人間は食べ物がなくても5週間は生きることができるが、空気がないと5分間しか生きることができないと言われている。水がない場合は、5日間以上は生き延びることはできないだろう。人間は水なしでは生きることができないので、古代より水が豊かな所で生活する傾向がある。

(is / people / said / it / that / can / for / survive / five / food, / weeks without / but / for / air / minutes without / only five). (without / you / water, / could / for / not / five / survive / more / than / days). (people / because / cannot / water, / live / ancient / without / since / times / have / they / tended / to / plentiful / live / is / where / water).

Reading Comprehension I

▶次の文章を読み，後の問いに答えなさい。 15

　　Arsene Lupin is the main character created ①(　　) French writer Maurice LeBlanc ②(　　) the early 20th century. Lupin is a gentleman thief, who is good ③(　　) wearing disguises. He is a nice and witty person and he doesn't harm the poor and innocent. In fact, he gives them gifts as acts of kindness. ⒶTo do this, he steals mainly from the rich and powerful who don't respect art or their treasures. Lupin is different from regular robbers, who steal from everybody and sometimes kill or hurt people getting in their way. ⒷBecause he sides with the weak and crushes the strong, he receives widespread support from people in many countries.
　　Lupin the Third, the Japanese familiar animated cartoon character, is named ④(　　) a grandchild of Arsene Lupin. For that reason, he doesn't murder for money and jewels.

注　wearing disguises 変装すること　　cartoon 漫画・アニメ

1 ▶（　）①〜④に適切な前置詞を書き入れなさい。

① (　　　　　　) French writer Maurice LeBlanc
② (　　　　　　) the early 20th century
③ who is good (　　　　　　) wearing disguises.
④ (　　　　　　) a grandchild of Arsene Lupin

2 ▶下線部ⒶⒷを日本文に直しなさい。

Ⓐ　To do this, he steals mainly from the rich and powerful

Ⓑ　Because he sides with the weak and crushes the strong, he receives widespread support from people in many countries.

Reading Comprehension II

▶次の文章を読み，後の問いに答えなさい。　　　　　　　　　　16

Rakugo is a form of traditional Japanese spoken entertainment. It first became popular among people of the merchant class "chonin," and also spread to the lower classes during the Edo period.

A single rakugo performer appears on stage and kneels on a cushion. The performer wears a traditional Japanese kimono and usually has nothing except two stage properties: a paper fan and a hand towel. The fan can be used to represent a variety of things, such as a pipe, chopsticks, a pen, a fishing pole or a cup. Sometimes it creates sound effects. The hand towel can be used for things like a letter, a book or an actual towel. The comic story, which the performer narrates, is usually in the form of a conversation between two or more characters. The storyteller plays the two or three roles fluently and switches from one character to another by changing his voice, accent, or expression and turning his head, so the audience can imagine the scene.

In the Meiji period, a British rakugo performer brought a lot of excitement to the audience. He was the first foreign-born rakugo perfomer, named Henry James Black, who adopted the stage name "Kairakutei Black." Everyone had a good laugh at hearing his comic tales and his fluent Edo dialect.

注　　kneel on a cushion 座布団に座る　　sound effects 効果音
　　　have a good laugh at ~ ～に大笑いする

1 ▶次の質問に英語で答えなさい。

(1) How many stage properties does the rakugo performer usually have?

　　_____

(2) What can a paper fan be used for?

　　_____

(3) How does the storyteller play two or three roles fluently?

　　_____

(4) Who was Kairakutei Black?

　　_____

(5) What was everyone laughing at?

　　_____

Chapter 6 形容詞・副詞と比較級

Grammar Check 🔵 17

1 ▶ 形容詞の限定・叙述用法
    1)   Alice is a **diligent** girl.（限定） 2) My uncle looks **young** for his age.（叙述）

2 ▶ 形容詞の語順（冠詞類→序数→数量→性状→大小・形状→色・新旧→材料所属）名詞
    3)   Would you try **these first ripe big** apples?

3 ▶ 数量形容詞
    4)   There are **many / a few / few** mistakes in his report.
    5)   We have **much / a little / little** time to decide what to do next.

4 ▶ 副詞の用法（①動詞・②形容詞・③他の副詞を修飾）
    6)   Ben **studies** English very **hard**. 7) She is **very busy**. 8) He drives **too fast**.

5 ▶ 副詞の位置
    形容詞・副詞を修飾する場合：ふつう被修飾語の前
    9)   You're **quite** right.
    動詞を修飾する場合：① 頻度・否定・② 様態・③ 時と場所を表す副詞の場合
    10)-1 She **sometimes** comes to see us.   （①：一般動詞の場合はその前）
    10)-2 He is **usually** free on Saturdays.   （①：be 動詞・助動詞の場合はその後）
    11)-1 Jill lived **happily** with Jack.   （②：自動詞の場合はその後）
    11)-2 She will answer the questions **easily**.   （②：他動詞の場合はふつう目的語の後）
    12)   There was a traffic accident **here yesterday**.（③：ふつう場所の副詞が先）

6 ▶ 原級・比較級・最上級を用いた比較表現
    13)   She is **not as** tall **as** her sister.
    14)   His boat is **five times as** big **as** mine. = His boat is **five times the** size **of** mine.
    15)   Tom works **as** hard **as** he **can**. = Tom works **as** hard **as possible**.
    16)   I spent **as much** money **as** he (did) in the amusement park yesterday.
    17)   Ned read **twice as many** books **as** I (did) last month.
    18)   Davis is **taller than** his brother. 19) Dogs are **more useful than** cats.
    20)   Alice can play tennis **much better than** I (can). ※他の強意語句には far, even 等。
    21)   There are **many more** pigs **than** people there.（複数名詞を伴って）「よりずっと多い」
    22)   Taro is **taller than any other** boy here. = Taro is the tallest of all the boys here.
    23)   Her bag is **less** heavy **than** mine. = Her bag is not as heavy as mine.
    24)   It is getting **colder and colder**.「だんだん～」
    25)   This is **the oldest** church here. 26) Lucy is **the most beautiful** of the five.
    27)   She is **happiest** when she has a date with Tom. ※同一人（物）に関する比較のとき。
    28)   He is **by far the best** here. ※他の強意語句：much(much the best), very(the very best)等。
    29)   He is **the second tallest** boy here.
    30)   He is **one of the most popular** actors here.

Exercises

A ▶ 次の英文の( )内から適語(句)を選びなさい。

1. In Japan we have (many / much) rain in June.
2. It is raining very (hardly / hard).
3. He doesn't have (some / any) money with him.
4. There is (a few / a little) milk in the bottle.
5. Taro looks (young / younger / the youngest) than Bill.
6. Which do you like (much / well / better), tea or coffee?
7. I can't speak French as (well / better / best) as Dick.
8. He studies (hard / harder / the hardest) of the five.

B ▶ 次の英文を例にならって書き換えなさい。

例 She plays the piano very well.　⇔ She is a very good pianist.
1. Henry speaks very carefully.　⇔ _____
2. Betty is a very hard worker.　⇔ _____
3. She can speak English very well.　⇔ _____

C ▶ 次の英文の( )内の語を正しく並べ替えなさい。

1. (must / clean / you / your / keep / room).
   _____
2. (Bill / for / late / sometimes / is / school).
   _____
3. (kind / was / the / very / girl / us / to).
   _____
4. (an / told / story / interesting / he / us).
   _____
5. Light travels (than / much / faster) sound.
   _____
6. Mt. Fuji is (other / higher / any / than) mountain in Japan.
   _____
7. This is (terrible / far / the / by / most) experience I have ever had.
   _____
8. I want to read (many / as / as / books) I can.
   _____

D ▶ 次の英文を日本文に直しなさい。

1. This box is five times as heavy as that one.　_____
2. Come as early as possible.　_____
3. He speaks English more fluently than she (does).　_____
4. The story became more and more interesting.　_____
5. This is one of the tallest buildings in the city.　_____

Composition

Vocabulary ▶ 語頭文字と文字数をヒントに綴りなさい。

01. 好奇心　　c-(9)　　02. 本能　　　i-(8)　　03. 無知の　　i-(8)　　04. 用心深い　c-(8)

05. 壮麗な　　s-(8)　　06. 信頼　　　r-(8)　　07. 乗り物　　c-(8)　　08. 目的地　　d-(11)

09. 投げる　　c-(4)　　10. 組み立てる c-(7)　　11. だます　　d-(7)　　12. 嫌悪　　　d-(7)

13. 予言者　　p-(7)　　14. 遭遇する　e-(9)　　15. 先祖　　　a-(8)　　16. だめにする s-(5)

17. 与える　　r-(6)　　18. 熟達者　　e-(6)　　19. 移民　　　i-(9)　　20. 専門家　　s-(10)

21. 正確な　　a-(8)　　22. 適当な　　a-(8)　　23. 力　　　　s-(8)　　24. それとなく言う i-(5)

25. 思いつく　c-(8)　　26. 観察する　o-(7)　　27. 解放　　　l-(10)　　28. 拷問　　　t-(7)

29. 奇数の　　o-(3)　　30. 調査する　s-(6)　　31. 微妙な　　s-(6)　　32. 奇妙な　　q-(5)

33. 理解する　c-(10)　 34. 工芸　　　c-(5)　　35. あいまいな o-(7)　　36. 誓約　　　p-(6)

37. 注目すべき n-(7)　 38. 規律　　　d-(10)　 39. 評価する　a-(10)　 40. 機能　　　f-(8)

Rearranging ▶ 次の日本文に合うように [ ] 内の語に**語頭文字が示された語**を加えて並べ替えなさい。

01. このエンジンはどこかおかしい。
    [(w　　　　) / with / there / this / is / engine / something].

02. 当然のことながら，彼女は彼に腹を立てた。
    [(n　　　　) / angry / him / she / with / got].

03. 私たちの作法のいくつかは彼らには奇妙に思われる。
    [(s　　　　) / of / are / to / some / manners / them / our].

04. 美とは，人間の理想のひとつである。
    [(b　　　　) / of / the / the / is / one / ideals / human].

05. 私は彼女ほど流暢に英語を話さない。
    [(f　　　　) / I / she / don't / does / as / as / English / speak].

06. その番組はますます面白くなってきている。
　　[(e　　　　) / that / is / and / program / more / more / getting].

07. 彼はうそをつくような人ではない。
　　[(l　　　　) / is / tell / the / a / he / man / lie / to].

Basic Composition ▶ (　)内の条件をヒントに英文に直しなさい。

01. 幸運なことに彼は重傷ではなかった。　　　(fortunately, seriously, (i　　) を用いて6語で)

02. あなたは，きっと，すばらしい通訳になるよ。　(I'm, you'll, (g　　) を用いて7語で)

03. 金持ちが必ずしも貧乏人より幸せとは限らない。　(the を2回用いて9語で)

04. 私の両親はもはや生きてはいない。　　　　(longer を用いて6語で)

05. 彼は千円しか持っていない。　　　　　　　(more を用いて8語で)

06. 私は彼を知れば知るほど彼が嫌いになった。　(more, less を用いて10語で)

07. 彼は自由な時間を最大限に利用した。　　　(made, most を用いて8語で)

Applied Composition ▶ 次の日本文に合うように，下の語(句)を並べ替えて正しい英文に直しなさい。

山あらしは大きな外敵から身を守るために硬く長いトゲを持っているが，それがときに不便になる場合がある。寒い冬の朝に，2匹の山あらしは体を温めるために，お互いに体をすり寄せるようにする。しかしながら，その山あらしが体をすり寄せ，近づけば近づくほど，トゲでお互いに傷つけ合ってしまい，すぐ離れてしまう。そのすり寄ったり離れたりという行動を繰り返していくうちにやがて，2匹の山あらしはほどよい距離を確立する。

(have / porcupines / stiff, / long / that / spines / help / defend / them / against / themselves / animals / larger). (their / are / spines, though, / for them / sometimes inconvenient). (winter / a cold / on / morning, / two / try / porcupines / will / keep warm / to / each other / to / nestle up / to). (however, / they / the closer / snuggle, / the more / each other / they / with / injure / their / spines, so / move / they / soon / apart). (this action / again / is repeated / and again, / until / establish / they / the proper / themselves / distance / between).

Reading Comprehension 1

▶次の文章を読み，後の問いに答えなさい。　　　　　　　　　18

　　Giraffes, the tallest animals on Earth, live in the dry savanna, or open woodlands, on the African continent. They can reach 530 centimeters tall, and they weigh ①(　　　) 1 ton. < enough / beat / are / strong / Giraffes' legs / to / lions >. Giraffes are vegetarians, so they eat leaves on trees using their long necks and tongues.
　　How long is a mother giraffe pregnant? The average pregnancy period is about 15 months. A giraffe gives birth standing up or walking because lying on the grass makes her an easy target for predators. A baby giraffe (calf), however, falls from a height of 2 meters to the ground. A newborn giraffe is about 180 cm tall and weighs about 100 kg. <u>A baby can stand up within 20 minutes and feed on its mother's milk soon after.</u> The mother giraffe stays close to her baby and protects her baby from predators. But when the mother needs to find water and food for her baby, she can leave her baby in a "nursery." In the "nursery," one or more female giraffes take turns guarding and caring for all their children. For a mother giraffe, to bring up her child with other female giraffes is ②(　　　) safer than raising it by herself.

　　注　　pregnant 妊娠した　　predator 肉食動物　　nursery 保育所

1 ▶ (　) ①②に次の日本文に合うように適切な語(句)を入れなさい。

① 「1トンもの」　→　(　　　　　　　　) 1 ton.
② 「はるかに安全」　→　(　　　　　　　　) safer than ...

2 ▶ < >内の語(句)を「キリンの脚はライオンに勝つほど強い」という意味になるように並べ替えなさい。

< enough / beat / are / strong / Giraffes' legs / to / lions >.

_____

_____

3 ▶ 下線部を日本文に直しなさい。

A baby can stand up within 20 minutes and feed on its mother's milk soon after.

_____

_____

Reading Comprehension II

▶次の文章を読み，後の問いに答えなさい。

Clint Eastwood is an American actor, movie director, producer, and also a musical composer. He won the Academy Award for Best Director twice for his work in the films *Unforgiven* (1992) and *Million Dollar Baby* (2004). He is the oldest winner of the Academy Award for Best Director, which he received at the age of 74. He became known for acting in the TV series *Rawhide* as a cowboy, and in the film *Dirty Harry* as a police inspector. It seems that he used to be better known as manly movie star than a film director.

Eastwood has been involved in more than 60 films. But in 2006, he made the bravest and most admirable attempt of them all. He made two films about the history of the Battle of Iwo Jima from both the American and the Japanese point of view: *Flags of Our Fathers* (2006) and *Letters From Iwo Jima* (2006). It may be said that Eastwood succeeded in making history not merely an issue of which side you are on, but an issue of how to view history itself. In other words, when we see both sides of something, we can be closer to the essence of that thing than just seeing it from one side.

注　musical composer 作曲家

1 ▶次の質問に英語で答えなさい。

(1) What does Clint Eastwood do?

(2) How many times did Clint Eastwood win the Academy Award for Best Director?

(3) What did Clint Eastwood become known for?

(4) What was his bravest and most admirable attempt?

(5) What did Eastwood succeed in?

Chapter 7　命令文・感嘆文

Grammar Check　🔵 20

1 ▶ 命令文

1) **Look** at the map of the city of Rome.
2) **Be** quiet here.
3) Waiter, please **give** me a cup of coffee.
4) **Don't speak** Japanese in this room.
5) **Don't be** late for school again.
6) **Let** me know where he lives.
7) **Let's** toss a coin to decide.
8) **Get up** early, **or** you will miss the train.
9) **Turn** to the right, **and** you will find the school.
10) **Let's not** talk about it.

2 ▶ What 感嘆文

11) **What a wonderful city** Rome is!
12) **What an interesting book** this is!
13) **What lovely flowers** those are!
14) **What wonderful hair** she has!
15) **What a waste!** 「何ともったいないことか」
16) **What a shame!** 「何と残念なことか」
17) **What a terrible thing to do!** 「何とひどいことをすることか」
18) **What luck!** 「何と運がいいことか」
19) **What nonsense!** 「何とばかばかしいことか」

3 ▶ How 感嘆文

20) **How foolish** I was!
21) **How beautifully** she is singing!
22) **How boring** his lectures are!
23) **How wonderful a city** Rome is!
24) **How careless** of you to do so! 「そんなことをするなんて，何と不注意なことか」
25) **How kind** of you to say so! 「そう言ってくれてありがとう」
26) **How** he has grown! 「何と大きくなったことか」
27) **How** she talks! 「何とよくしゃべることか」
28) **How it snows** here in winter! 「何と雪が多いことか」

Exercises

A ▶ 次の英文を命令文に直しなさい。

1. You are silent here.

2. You don't mix these together.

3. You will be back here by eleven o'clock.

4. We will play tennis after school.

5. We will not go there.

B ▶ 次の英文を感嘆文に直しなさい。

1. That is a very amusing story.

2. These are very interesting books.

3. The athlete is running very fast.

4. You look very pale.

5. You have very good pictures.

6. It is very foolish of you to do such a thing.

C ▶ 次の日本文を(　)内の語(句)を用いて英文に直しなさい。

1. 私にもっと食べ物をください。　　　　(please, food)

2. 泣くな。手伝うから。　　　　(cry, help)

3. ドライブに行きましょう。　　　　(a drive)

4. あなたは何と素敵な本を書いたことか。　　　　(nice, written)

5. あなたは何と美しいバラを持っていることか。　　　　(roses)

6. これは何と古い切手だこと。　　　　(old stamp)

7. その花は何といい香りがすることか。　　　　(smells)

8. 風は何と強く吹くことか。　　　　(blow hard)

9. 彼は何と利口なことか。　　　　(clever)

Composition

Vocabulary ▶ 語頭文字と文字数をヒントに綴りなさい。

01. 容易さ	f-(8)	02. 努力	e-(6)	03. 気づく, 掲示	n-(6)	04. 感謝する	a-(11)
05. 本物の	g-(7)	06. 協定	t-(6)	07. 長所	m-(5)	08. 復習する	r-(6)
09. 祝う	c-(9)	10. 人を誤らせる	m-(10)	11. 犠牲	v-(6)	12. 恐怖	t-(6)
13. 恥じて	a-(7)	14. お世辞を言う	f-(7)	15. 意識して	c-(9)	16. 喜ぶ	r-(7)
17. 思い出させる	r-(6)	18. 苦難	h-(8)	19. 恐怖	h-(6)	20. 上品な	d-(6)
21. 故意の	d-(10)	22. 絶望的な	d-(9)	23. 汚染	p-(9)	24. 親しい	i-(8)
25. みじめな	m-(9)	26. 神聖な	h-(4)	27. 容易	e-(4)	28. 困窮	d-(8)
29. 抑制	r-(9)	30. なだめる	s-(6)	31. 反対する	o-(6)	32. 自白する	c-(7)
33. あこがれる	y-(5)	34. 熱望する	a-(6)	35. 寂しい	s-(8)	36. 疑う	s-(7)
37. 無視する	i-(6)	38. 怠慢	n-(7)	39. 大事にする	c-(7)	40. 疲労	f-(7)

Rearranging ▶ 次の日本文に合うように（　）内の語(句)に **1語を加えて**並べ替えなさい。

01. Ann は何とすぐれた運動選手なのでしょう。　(is / fine / an / Ann / athlete)!

02. 彼女たちは何と親切な少女たちだろう。　(girls / are / kind / they)!

03. 彼の身なりは何と滑稽だったことか。　(clothes / were / ridiculous / his)!

04. 彼は私に何と難しい質問をしたことか。　(difficult / asked / a / me / question / he)!

05. 学校に遅れてはいけません。　(be / for / school / late).

06. 来週の金曜日にパーティーを開きましょう。　(next / have / party / Friday / a).

07. 他人をからかうのはやめましょう。　(others / make / of / let's / fun).

08. 発信人がわからない限り，決して添付ファイルを開いてはいけない。

(an attachment / the sender / you / open / know / unless).

___

Basic Composition ▶ (　)内の条件をヒントに英文に直しなさい。

01. 弱者に親切でやさしくありなさい。　　　　　　（be, gentle, to を用いて7語で）

02. あまり長くビデオゲームをしてはならない。　　（very を用いて6語で）

03. この川では絶対に一人で泳いではいけない。　　（never を用いて6語で）

04. しばらく休憩を取りましょう。　　　　　　　　（let's, while を用いて7語で）

05. 今夜その会合に出席するのはやめましょう。　　（let's を用いて6語で）

06. マサコははなんと流暢に英語を話せるのでしょう。（fluently を用いて6語で）

07. あれは何と長い橋なのでしょう。　　　　　　　（6語で）

08. 子供たちは上の部屋で何と大騒ぎをしているのでしょう。（upstairs room を用いて12語で）

Applied Composition ▶ 次の日本文に合うように，下の語(句)を並べ替えて正しい英文に直しなさい。

ワインの瓶の上げ底をもう一度よく見て下さい。ワインの量を減らすために如何にうまくもくろまれているのでしょう。しかし，それは事実ではありません。美味しい味を出すために樽の中で長い時間熟成させなければなりません。熟成中には，ワインから澱が出てきます。その澱を取り除くためにワインは別の樽へと繰り返し移され，瓶に詰められコルクで栓をされます。その後も熟成を続け，さらに澱をもたらします。上げ底はその澱が外に流れ出るのを防ぐようになっています。

(have / bottle / another / good look / bottom of / at / the raised / a wine). (skillfully designed / to decrease / how / the quantity / it is / of wine)! (the case / that / not / is). (in casks / wine / has to / be / its taste / long / matured / to improve). (during / it produces / maturation / lees). (to remove / the lees, / in order / the wine / is poured / repeatedly / is bottled / into other / casks and / and corked). (after / it / that, / will still / continue / to mature / more lees / and produce). (the raised / the bottle / the lees / bottom / prevents / flowing / from / out of).

Reading Comprehension I

▶次の文章を読み，後の問いに答えなさい。　　　　　　　　　　　21

You may have heard of the word "biological clock." Generally, this word is most often used as "life rhythm." But we all actually have clock genes in our bodies. There are an equal number of clock genes and body cells, numbering about 60 trillion. What an astonishing number of cells we have!

Many scientists have been engaging in research about biological clock and analyzing the mechanism of it. It seems that the main biological clock is located in the brain. The main clock's signals are delivered to biological clocks throughout the body: "Get up!," "Breakfast is ready. Please eat!" "Don't stay up too late!" or "Please go to bed."

Animals and plants, as well as humans, also have biological clocks. The clocks are responsible for the daily and yearly rhythms of all living things. These are believed to be able to help in the treatment of all kinds of diseases, especially depression and sleeplessness.

注　biological clock 体内時計　clock gene 時計遺伝子　an equal number A and B　AとB同数
trillion 1兆　treatment 治療　depression うつ病

1 ▶次の質問に英語で答えなさい。

(1) What is most often used as "life rhythm?"

(2) How many clock genes do we have?

(3) What have many scientists been doing?

(4) Don't plants have biological clocks?

(5) What are biological clocks responsible for?

Reading Comprehension II

▶次の文章を読み，後の問いに答えなさい。　　　　　　　　　　　22

People in other countries generally think the Japanese are polite. A guidebook for travelers provides Japanese customs and manners. Let me introduce several of them.
- Don't enter a house with your shoes on.
- Avoid blowing your nose in front of other people.
- You should not eat while standing or walking in the street or in the house.
- Don't point your finger, feet or chopsticks at people.
- Don't interrupt people when they are speaking or thinking of a response.
- Please say "itadakimasu" before eating. This word means "I thankfully receive." After eating, Japanese say "gochisosama deshita," which roughly means "Thank you for the delicious meal."
- Don't pass food directly from your chopsticks to another's. This is a Buddhist funeral tradition.
- Don't use chopsticks to pull plates or bowls closer to you.
- Don't talk to someone with your hands in your pockets.
- Please try not to yawn, or cover your mouth if you must.

It is said that modern Japanese manners originated from the style of bushi's wife or "bushido."

注　　Buddhist 仏教の　funeral 葬式　bushi: warrior　bushido: Japanese chivalry

1 ▶次の質問に英語で答えなさい。

(1) What do people in other countries think about the Japanese?

_____

(2) Should we avoid blowing our noses in front of other people?

_____

(3) What does "itadakimasu" mean?

_____

(4) Why is it wrong to pass food directly from your chopsticks to another's?

_____

(5) What are modern Japanese manners said to have originated from?

_____

Chapter 8　不定詞

Grammar Check　　23

1 ▶ 不定詞の基本的用法

名詞的用法

1) **To walk** is healthy exercise.（主語として）
2) I want **to travel** abroad.（目的語として）
3) My dream is **to help** sick and poor people.（補語として）

形容詞的用法

4) I have some friends **to support** me.
5) There is no one **to help** him in the whole world.
6) I want something **to drink**.

副詞的用法

7) I got up early **to catch** the first train.（目的）
8) I am glad **to hear** the news.（原因・理由）
9) He awoke **to find** himself in a strange room.（結果）

2 ▶ 不定詞に関する基本事項および慣用表現

10) **It** is good for the health **to keep** early hours.（形式主語によって文尾に）
11) I found **it** difficult **to solve** the problem.（形式目的語によって文尾に）
12) Dave often **asks** me **to help** him with his homework.（目的語＋不定詞）
    = Dave often says to me, "Please help me with my homework."
13) Do you know **what to do** next?（疑問詞＋不定詞）
    = Do you know what you should do next?
14) She was **too tired to walk** any farther.
    = She was so tired that she couldn't walk any farther.
15) He is tall **enough to touch** the ceiling.
    = He is so tall that he can touch the ceiling.
16) He told me **not to open** the door.（不定詞の否定）
    = He said to me, "Don't open the door."
17) I **saw** him **enter** the restaurant with his wife.（知覚動詞の後の原形不定詞）
    → He was seen **to enter** the restaurant with his wife.
18) They **made** me **work** all day long.（使役動詞の後の原形不定詞）
    → I was made **to work** all day long.
19) You don't have to go there if you don't want **to**.（代不定詞）
    = You don't have to go there if you don't want **to go there**.
20) You had better start at once.「～するほうがいい」

Exercises

A ▶ 次の英文を日本文に直しなさい。

1. There was no time to lose.
2. To get up early, you must go to bed early.
3. I found it difficult to do so.
4. Will you lend me something to write with?
5. He was very disappointed to hear the result.

B ▶ 次の1〜3の文中の不定詞と同じ用法のものを下から2つずつ選び記号で答えなさい。

1. His only fault is to talk too much.　　　(　) (　)
2. Please give me something to drink.　　　(　) (　)
3. I was surprised to hear the news of his death.　(　) (　)

> a) Please come to see us next Sunday.
> b) He has no house to live in.
> c) Please teach me how to cook.
> d) It is my great pleasure to read books after supper.
> e) He grew up to be a great scientist.
> f) The best way to master English is practice.

C ▶ 次の各組の英文の意味が同じになるように (　) 内に適切な語を書き入れなさい。

1. They saw her wash the dishes.
   She was (　　　　) (　　　　) wash the dishes.
2. She said to her son, "Don't swim in the river."
   She told her son (　　　　) (　　　　) swim in the river.
3. He is so rich that he can buy a yacht.
   He is rich (　　　　) (　　　　) buy a yacht.
4. The dress is so expensive that she cannot buy it.
   The dress is (　　　　) expensive (　　　　) her (　　　　) buy.

D ▶ 次の日本文を (　) 内の語(句)を用いて英文に直しなさい。

1. 私はそれを聞いてとてもうれしい。　　(glad, hear that)

2. 彼の仕事はバスを運転することだ。　　(job, drive)

3. この部屋には座る椅子がない。　　(no chairs, on)

4. この英和辞典は使いやすい。　　(easy, use)

49

Composition

Vocabulary ▶ 語頭文字と文字数をヒントに綴りなさい。

01. 全体で　　　a-(10)　02. その上に　b-(7)　　03. 農業　　　a-(11)　04. 知恵　　　w-(6)

05. 間もなく　p-(9)　　06. 名声　　　r-(10)　07. ゆるい　　l-(5)　　08. 逆らう　　r-(6)

09. それゆえに　t-(9)　10. 外見上の　a-(8)　　11. 正当性　　j-(7)　　12. 美人　　　b-(6)

13. このように　t-(4)　14. 魅力的な　a-(10)　15. 利益　　　b-(7)　　16. 価値　　　v-(5)

17. とにかく　　a-(6)　18. 安全　　　s-(8)　　19. 事故　　　a-(8)　　20. 共有する　s-(5)

21. すなわち　　n-(6)　22. 解決する　r-(7)　　23. 災害　　　d-(8)　　24. 分かれた　s-(8)

25. 競争する　　c-(7)　26. 壮大な　　m-(11)　27. 光景　　　s-(9)　　28. 斬新さ　　n-(7)

29. 本質　　　　e-(7)　30. かすかな　f-(5)　　31. 獲得する　a-(7)　　32. 整える　　a-(7)

33. 浅薄な　　　s-(11)　34. 念入りの　e-(9)　35. 新紀元　　e-(5)　　36. 避ける　　a-(5)

37. 気の利いた　s-(5)　38. 美徳　　　v-(6)　　39. 空いている　v-(6)　40. 時代　　　e-(3)

Rearranging ▶ 次の日本文に合うように（　）内の語に **1語を加えて**並べ替えなさい。

01. 彼は私にこの部屋を使わないように言った。　　(me / to / he / room / told / use / this).

02. この小説は1日で読めるほど短い。　　　　　　(is / to / one / this / short / day / novel / read / in).

03. 彼女は私に1時間後に戻ってくると約束した。　(me / in / she / hour / to / an / back / be).

04. 秋は読書に最良の季節だ。　　　　　　　　　　(is / read / the / to / season / best).

05. 出かける前に窓を閉めるのを忘れないように。　(to / leaving / don't / window / close / before / the).

06. 切符をどこで買えばよいのか教えて下さい。　　(tell / buy / please / ticket / me / a / to).

07. そんなことをするなんて、彼は狂っているに違いない。　(he / mad / a / must / thing / be / do / to).

08. 彼は電車に乗り遅れたようだ。　　　　　　　(the / to / missed / he / train / seems).

09. 彼女は外国に行ってしまったと思われた。　　(abroad / was / she / to / gone / have).

10. 何か冷たい飲み物をください。　　　　　　　(me / cold / to / please / drink / give).

Basic Composition ▶ (　　)内の条件をヒントに英文に直しなさい。

01. 私は登りたいからその山に登ったのだ。　　　(because, to を用いて 8 語で)

02. 最寄のコンビニにはどうやって行けばよいのか教えていただけませんか。　(could, get を用いて 12 語で)

03. 急ぐ必要はありません。　　　　　　　　　　(there, no, be を用いて 9 語で)

04. 私はスキーに行ったが，脚を折っただけだった。(, only を用いて 8 語で)

05. 言うまでもなくバスは遅れた。　　　　　　　(needless を用いて 7 語で)

06. 早寝早起きは健康によい。　　　　　　　　　(it, keep を用いて 10 語で)

07. 彼女にはそんなに腹を立てる理由は何もない。(reason, angry を用いて 8 語で)

08. あなたが禁煙するのは無理だろう。　　　　　(will, give を用いて 10 語で)

09. あなたの祝電をもらってとてもうれしかった。(congratulatory telegram を用いて 9 語で)

Applied Composition ▶ 次の日本文に合うように，下の語(句)を並べ替えて正しい英文に直しなさい。

郵便料金は高すぎた。貧しい人たちは払えなかった。ローランド・ヒル卿 (Sir Rowland Hill) は，郵便制度を変えるために何をすればよいかわかっていた。彼は，政府に制度を改善するよう要請した。このようにして，ペニー・ブラックという最初の郵便切手が 1840 年に英国で誕生した。

(the / too / was / postage / high). (it / couldn't / people / pay / poor). (what / knew / Sir Rowland Hill / the postal / to change / to do / system). (the Government / asked / he / better / the system / to make). (in / the / this way, / called / stamp / first postage / in Britain / was born / the "Penny Black" / in / 1840).

Reading Comprehension I

▶次の文章を読み，後の問いに答えなさい。　24

Have you ever been to a Halloween party? Halloween is an annual celebration on October 31st. It is thought that Halloween originated with the Celts. For the Celts, October 31st was the eve of the New Year and Samhain (November 1st) when ghosts, evil spirits, witches, and fairies were especially active. So the Celts disguised themselves as demons or witches to protect themselves from real demons or witches. The jack o' lantern is also a famous Celtic tradition. The Celts used to use a carved turnip, but after Halloween reached America a carved pumpkin became popular. ① (The jack o' lantern is lit and placed outside doorways to keep evil spirits away.)

These days, Halloween is popular in Japan regardless of religion or cultural background. ② (It's fun for many people to get dressed up and go to Halloween parties.) ③ (They seem to be excited to dress up for Halloween.)

注　Samhain ケルト民族の新年であり秋の収穫祭　evil spirit 悪霊
　　disguise ~ ~を変装させる　jack o' lantern カボチャちょうちん　turnip カブ

1 ▶（　）①〜③を日本文に直し，それぞれの下線部が不定詞の何用法か答えなさい。

① The jack o' lantern is lit and placed outside of doorways to keep evil spirits away.

_____

_____

用法（　　　　　　）

② It's fun for many people to get dressed up and go to Halloween parties.

_____

_____

用法（　　　　　　）

③ They seem to be excited to dress up for Halloween.

_____

_____

用法（　　　　　　）

Reading Comprehension II

▶次の文章を読み，後の問いに答えなさい。

The problem of global warming remains a central concern for people all over the world. Carbon dioxide (CO_2) is believed to be the major cause of global warming. We have to solve the global warming crisis to preserve the environment. What produces carbon dioxide? The main cause is a large number of automobiles. To drive cars makes global warming worse. But the modern hybrid cars consume less gasoline than conventional cars, so eco-friendly hybrid cars are rapidly gaining popularity.

Many automobile companies are hastening the development and research of other ecologically clean cars. One of them is the hydrogen-powered car. There are two types of hydrogen vehicles. One is a vehicle that directly uses hydrogen as fuel. The other is a vehicle that runs on electrical energy derived from the chemical reaction between hydrogen and oxygen (Fuel Cell Vehicle). These cars can reduce the emissions of carbon dioxide and other greenhouse gases considerably. At this time, hydrogen cars have both advantages and disadvantages. Hydrogen fuel does not occur on the Earth naturally, so we must produce enough hydrogen fuel to power cars. The developers of hydrogen cars are struggling to find a safe method of production and a way to store the hydrogen fuel.

注　carbon dioxide 二酸化炭素　preserve 保護する　hydrogen 水素　fuel 燃料
emission 排出　greenhouse gas 温室効果ガス　considerably 大幅に

1 ▶次の質問に英語で答えなさい。

(1) What causes global warming?

(2) What makes global warming worse?

(3) How does a Fuel Cell Vehicle run?

(4) What can hydrogen-powered cars do?

(5) Does hydrogen fuel occur on Earth naturally?

Chapter 9　動名詞と分詞

Grammar Check　　　　　　　　　　　　　　　　　26

動名詞

1 ▶ 文の主要素（主語，補語，目的語）

1) **Seeing** is **believing**.
2) My hobby is **collecting** stamps.
3) Her brother stopped **smoking** two months ago.
   cf. I stopped **to smoke**.（修飾語）
4) I like **swimming**.
   cf. I like **to swim**.（「～したい」と一時的な場合もある）
5) **It** is no use **crying** over spilt milk.（It = crying …）

2 ▶ 前置詞の目的語

6) We usually begin class by **reviewing** the last lesson.
7) How about **going** on a picnic?
8) I'm looking forward to **seeing** you soon.

3 ▶ 名詞を修飾…「名詞 for 動名詞」と解釈

9) This is a **sleeping** car. (= a car for sleeping)
10) He happened to meet her in the **waiting** room.
11) She got a can of orange juice from the **vending** machine.

4 ▶ 動名詞を目的語にとる動詞

12) You should **practice speaking** English every day.
13) I **missed watching** the TV program last night.
14) He **suggested playing** outside.
    = He suggested that we should play outside.
    ※他に，admit, avoid, enjoy, escape, finish, mind, put off, stop など

現在分詞と過去分詞

1 ▶ 分詞の限定用法（前置と後置）

15)-1　A **drowning** man will catch at a straw.
15)-2　A **lost** chance will never come again.
16)-1　Who is the girl **standing** next to Della?
16)-2　The dinner **cooked** by Father was very delicious.

2 ▶ 分詞の叙述用法（主格補語・目的格補語として）

17)-1　Dick stood **talking** with Beth in the train.
17)-2　He looked **worried** about his health.
18)-1　I saw him **watering** the flowers.
18)-2　I heard my name **called**.

Exercises

A ▶ 次の英文の下線部に（　）内の語を動名詞または分詞に直して書き入れなさい。

1. They enjoyed _____ a baseball game on TV.　　　(watch)
2. There is no _____ room in this building.　　　(smoke)
3. Her job is _____ vegetables.　　　(sell)
4. She is good at _____ the guitar.　　　(play)
5. My son went out without _____ goodbye.　　　(say)
6. Who is that _____ boy?　　　(cry)
7. There is a _____ watch on the desk.　　　(break)
8. Look at the boy _____ in the river.　　　(swim)
9. I have a car _____ in Germany.　　　(make)
10. The dog came _____ across the street.　　　(run)

B ▶ 次の英文の（　）内の語(句)を正しく並べ替えなさい。

1. My (hear / surprised / news / father / the / looked / to).
   _____

2. We (looking / for / at / kept / other / a / each) while.
   _____

3. There (standing / the doorway / is / in / someone).
   _____

4. You (be / water / the / careful / boiling / must / with).
   _____

5. The (my father's / is / by / washed / car / Tom).
   _____

6. (a letter / is / easy / in English / writing / not).
   _____

7. My (model planes / hobby / brother's / making / is).
   _____

8. (being / proud / born / I / Japanese / am / of).
   _____

C ▶ 次の日本文を（　）内の語を用いて英文に直しなさい。

1. 彼は私にフランス語で書かれた手紙を見せた。　　　(showed)
   _____

2. 私は夕食前に宿題をし終えた。　　　(doing, dinner)
   _____

3. 彼女はあなたから便りをもらうことを楽しみに待っている。　　　(looking, hearing)
   _____

55

Composition

Vocabulary ▶ 語頭文字と文字数をヒントに綴りなさい。

01. できごと　i-(8)　02. 地方の　l-(5)　03. 月の　l-(5)　04. 用意する　p-(7)

05. に値する　d-(7)　06. 姿勢　a-(8)　07. 保証する　a-(6)　08. 品物　a-(7)

09. 識別する　d-(11)　10. 試み　t-(5)　11. 関係させる　r-(6)　12. 事業　e-(10)

13. 住む（他動詞）i-(7)　14. 細部　d-(6)　15. 保証する　g-(9)　16. 勤勉な　i-(11)

17. に似ている　r-(8)　18. 退屈　b-(7)　19. 誓う　s-(5)　20. 工業の　i-(10)

21. 違う　d-(6)　22. 展示する　d-(7)　23. 交替　s-(5)　24. スタッフ　s-(5)

25. 巻き込む　i-(7)　26. 声を出す　u-(5)　27. 局面　a-(6)　28. 商業　c-(8)

29. 警報　a-(5)　30. みごとな　a-(9)　31. 人間性　h-(8)　32. ふるまう　b-(6)

33. 妨げる　p-(7)　34. 冷淡な　c-(6)　35. 委員会　c-(9)　36. 描写する　d-(8)

37. 確信させる　c-(8)　38. 適度な　m-(8)　39. 代表（者）r-(14)　40. 探偵　d-(9)

Rearranging ▶ 次の日本文に合うように（　）内の語に **1語を加えて**並べ替えなさい。

01. 彼らは全員たのしく試合を観戦した。（ the / all / game / enjoyed / they).

02. 彼は私がそこへ行くべきだと言い張った。(me / there / he / going / insisted).

03. この湖で泳ぐ際は気をつけなさい。(in / in / be / lake / careful / this).

04. 彼のことを気の毒に思わざるをえない。(for / I / him / sorry / cannot / feeling).

05. その事実を否定できない。(the / there / denying / is / fact).

06. 劇場で財布を盗まれた。(I / my / in / had / the / wallet / theater).

07. 長く待たせ続けてごめんなさい。(I'm / you / have / long / kept / to / sorry).

08. 大変疲れを感じたので，ひと休みした。　(tired, / I / rest / a / very / took).

09. 天候が許せば，今週末体育祭があります。
(have / day / this / we / sports / weather / will / weekend, / a).

Basic Composition ▶ (　)内の条件をヒントに英文に直しなさい。

01. 彼らは落ち葉を道端に掃き寄せている。　　　　(side, road を用いて11語で)

02. 私は幼年期に車にはねられたことを覚えている。　(hit, my を用いて10語で)

03. その本を取っていただけませんか。　　　　　　(mind, handing を用いて7語で)

04. おいでいただけないのは残念です。　　　　　　(it, disappointing, me を用いて8語で)

05. 何と言ってよいかわからなかったので，彼は黙っていた。(knowing, kept を用いて8語で)

06. 昨日は天気がよかったので，私たちはハイキングに行った。(being を用いて8語で)

07. 一般的に言って，早起きは三文の得。　　　　　(generally, catches を用いて8語で)

08. 私たちは黒のネクタイをして葬式に出る。　　　(attend, wearing, ties を用いて6語で)

Applied Composition ▶ 次の日本文に合うように，下の語(句)を並べ替えて正しい英文に直しなさい。

日本は，1994年に「高齢化社会」から「高齢社会」に突入した。その年に日本の高齢率—全人口に占める65歳以上の割合—が14%を超えたからである。社会は，高齢者が人口の7%以上を占めるようになると「高齢化社会」とみなされ，その率が14%を超えたとき「高齢社会」と言われる。

(from / to / in / Japan / changed / an "aging society" / an "aged society" / 1994). (was / that / the year / "aged ratio" / that / the nation's / older / of people / —the percentage / aged sixty-five / in the population / —topped fourteen). (as / a society / an aging society / is regarded / when / the aged / the population, / 7% of / exceed / when / an aged society / and as / that percentage / exceeds / 14%).

Reading Comprehension 1

▶次の文章を読み，後の問いに答えなさい。　　　　　　　　　　　27

UNESCO manages Intangible Cultural Heritage to support and preserve the untouchable aspects of culture, such as songs, performing arts, social customs or traditional skills.

Washoku, traditional Japanese dietary culture, was placed on the UNESCO list of Intangible Cultural Heritage in 2013. UNESCO recognized *washoku*'s spirit of respect for nature, as Japanese chefs use seasonable vegetables and flowers. ① Japanese foods are worth seeing and are famous around the world for being healthy food with a delicate taste.

② These days we can see people from many countries eating all kinds of Japanese dishes regularly, such as sushi, tempura, Ⓐ (pickle) plums, simmered dishes, and so on. ③ It is said that eating noodles in the Japanese way is difficult for them, because they are not comfortable making loud Ⓑ (slurp) noises.

注　be placed on the UNESCO list of Intangible Cultural Heritage ユネスコの世界無形文化遺産に登録される　simmer コトコト煮る　slurp 音をたてて食べる

1 ▶下線部①〜③を日本文に直しなさい。

① Japanese foods are worth seeing

② These days we can see people from many countries eating all kinds of Japanese dishes regularly

③ It is said that eating noodles in the Japanese way is difficult for them

2 ▶（　）Ⓐ Ⓑ の動詞を適切な形に直しなさい。

Ⓐ　（　　　　　　　） plums

Ⓑ　making loud （　　　　　　　） noises

Reading Comprehension II

▶次の文章を読み，後の問いに答えなさい。　　　　　　　　　　　28

Cricket is a bat-and-ball sport played on an egg-shaped field with two teams of eleven players each. Cricket was first played in England and it soon grew into England's national sport. It is popular chiefly in the Commonwealth countries, including Australia, New Zealand and India. Despite never catching on in Japan, it is now played in over 100 countries, and is the second most popular sport behind soccer. The fans look forward to the beginning of the cricket season each year.

Cricket is regarded as the origin of baseball, but there are many differences between the two sports. In cricket, the man throwing the ball is called the "bowler," while the man trying to hit the ball is known as the "batsman." The bowler must throw the ball with his arm straightened, and the batsman can hit the ball in any direction.

A Cricket match can last six hours a day, over a period of up to five days, so players have many breaks for tea and lunch. Cricket is known for its grace and sportsmanship. Therefore it is considered crucial for public school students, in order to develop healthy bodies and minds.

注　the Commonwealth countries 英国連邦　crucial 不可欠な

1 ▶次の質問に英語で答えなさい。

(1) What shape is a cricket field?

_____

(2) Where is cricket chiefly popular?

_____

(3) What is cricket regarded as?

_____

(4) How does the bowler throw the ball?

_____

(5) Why is cricket considered crucial for public school students?

_____

Chapter 10　各種疑問文・It の特別用法

Grammar Check 　29

各種疑問文

1 ▶ 付加疑問文（be 動詞・助動詞）
1) Tom is a tall boy, **isn't he?**
2) Nancy isn't his sister, **is she?**
3) Kazuo can swim fast, **can't he?**
4) This is a good ballpoint pen, **isn't it?**
5) There is a big hotel on the hill, **isn't there?** （主語は a big hotel）

2 ▶ 付加疑問文（一般動詞）
6) Keiko likes playing tennis very much, **doesn't she?**
7) Ben doesn't like sweet peppers, **does he?**
8) Ken and Akiko went on a picnic yesterday, **didn't they?**
9) He walks very fast, **doesn't he?**　Yes, he does. / No, he doesn't.
10) Be quiet, **will you?** / Let's go there, **shall we?**

3 ▶ 間接疑問文
11) I know **who he is**.
12) I don't know **why you called me**.
13) **When** do you think **Tom will come**?

It の特別用法

1 ▶ 天候・距離・明暗などを表す it
14) **It** is fine today.
15) **It** is about two miles from this park to my house.
16) **It** gets dark here before five in winter.

2 ▶ 時刻・月日・季節などを表す it
17) **It** is summer here in Japan now.
18) What day of the month is **it** today?　**It** is November 3.
19) What time is **it** by your watch?　**It** is eight o'clock.

3 ▶ 形式主語・目的語の it
20)-1 **It** is fun **to** swim in the sea.
20)-2 **It** is easy **for** you **to** answer the question.
21) I found **it** important **to** study English every day.

Exercises

A▶次の英文が付加疑問文になるように下線部に適切な語(句)を書き入れなさい。

1. Mike and Tom love little animals, _____ ?
2. Your father drove the car, _____ ?
3. Tom was swimming in the pool, _____ ?
4. Mother didn't play the violin, _____ ?
5. There are some boys in the playground, _____ ?

B▶次の英文の( )内の語(句)を正しく並べ替えなさい。

1. (what / you / Yuki / do / know / wants)?
   _____
2. We don't (didn't / you / why / to school / know / come) yesterday.
   _____
3. (me / lives / tell / will / where / you / he)?
   _____
4. (got / tell / can / he / you / me / how / here)?
   _____

C▶次の英文を日本文に直しなさい。

1. It is a quarter to ten.
   _____
2. It is two kilometers from here to the station.
   _____
3. It was very windy yesterday.
   _____
4. It is completely natural for her to say so.
   _____
5. It is getting colder tonight.
   _____

D▶次の日本文に合うように下線部に適切な語を書き入れなさい。

1. ここから駅まで距離にしてどのくらいありますか。
   _____ far is _____ from here to the station?
2. 10時半です。
   _____ _____ ten thirty. = _____ _____ _____ past _____ .
3. 歴史の本を読むのはとてもおもしろい。
   _____ is very _____ _____ read a history book.
4. 梅雨にはたくさん雨が降る。
   _____ rains a lot in the rainy season.
5. その問題を解くのは彼女にとって難しい。
   _____ is difficult _____ her _____ solve the problem.

Composition

Vocabulary ▶ 語頭文字と文字数をヒントに綴りなさい。

01. 探検する	e-(7)	02. 快適な	c-(11)	03. 国家	n-(6)	04. 捕らえる	c-(7)
05. 尋ねる	i-(7)	06. 便利な	c-(10)	07. 世代	g-(10)	08. 動かす	o-(7)
09. 調べる	i-(7)	10. 気に入りの	f-(8か9)	11. 軍隊	m-(8)	12. 敵	e-(5)
13. 注目すべき	r-(10)	14. あざける	r-(8)	15. 聴衆	a-(8)	16. 謝罪する	a-(9)
17. 批判的な	c-(8)	18. 慈善	c-(7)	19. 取り付ける	a-(6)	20. 基礎	f-(10)
21. 金銭上の	f-(9)	22. ことわざ	p-(7)	23. 剣	s-(5)	24. ゆりかご	c-(6)
25. 基本的な	f-(11)	26. 国際的な	i-(13)	27. 嘆く	l-(6)	28. 養う	n-(7)
29. 性格	c-(9)	30. 傾向	t-(5)	31. 遅らせる	d-(5)	32. (米)電気製品	a-(9)
33. 精神の	m-(6)	34. 慈悲深い	m-(8)	35. 移植する	t-(10)	36. 道具	i-(10)
37. 気高い	n-(5)	38. 日課,日常の	r-(7)	39. 模造する	i-(7)	40. 買う	p-(8)

Rearranging ▶ 次の日本文に合うように( )内の語に **1語を加えて**並べ替えなさい。

01. あなたはどうやって通学しているの。電車で。　　(go / school / do / to / you)? By train.

02. 彼女はカナダ人ですか，それともアメリカ人ですか。　(a / an / she / American / Canadian / is)?

03. あなたのお兄さんはスキーができますよね。　　　(can / brother / ski, / he / your)?

04. Alice はコーヒーが好きではありませんね。　　　(doesn't / she / like / coffee, / Alice)?

05. 誰がそこに住んでいるか知っていますか。　　　　(you / lives / know / there / do)?

06. あなたは彼がどこに住んでいると思いますか。　　(think / lives / you / he / do)?

07. 招待してくださってありがとうございます。　　　(is / of / to / me / very / you / kind / invite).

08. 彼がそこにいたのは明らかだ。　　　　　　　　(is / that / was / evident / he / there).

09. 悪いのは Tom です。　　　　　　　　　　　　(blame / that / is / is / Tom / to).

Basic Composition ▶ (　　)内の条件をヒントに英文に直しなさい。

01. 言葉の力を理解することは大切だと思う。　　　(it, speech を用いて 10 語で)

02. 来たい人は誰でも歓迎されるだろう。　　　　　(whoever, welcome を用いて 7 語で)

03. どちらへ行ったらいいのかわからない。　　　　(I, don't, way を用いて 8 語で)

04. 来たい時はいつでも来てください。　　　　　　(can, to を用いて 7 語で)

05. テニスをしましょうよ。　　　　　　　　　　　(shall を用いた付加疑問文で 5 語で)

06. ペンをどこに置いたかな。　　　　　　　　　　(wonder を用いた現在完了形の文で 8 語で)

07. ぜひ我が家にお越しください。　　　　　　　　(why を用いた疑問文で 7 語で)

Applied Composition ▶ 次の日本文に合うように，下の語(句)を並べ替えて正しい英文に直しなさい。

虹は何色ですか。日本人ならたいてい7色と答えるでしょう。外国人の中には6色と答える人もいます。一般的に，日本人が7色と言うのは7色すべてを識別するからです。他方，それらの外国人の場合は，往々にして紫と藍を区別しないのです。だから，7色でなく6色と答えるのです。

(how / colors / many / does / have / a rainbow)? (most / say / seven colors / Japanese / people / it / would / that / has). (foreigners / six colors / say / some / that / rainbows / have). (Japanese / a rainbow / people / generally / say / seven colors / that / has / because / they / colors / tend to / from / differentiate / all / of these / one another). (those / don't differentiate / foreigners, / on the / other hand, / often / violet / between / and indigo). (as / are apt / a result, / they / to say / not seven / that / a rainbow / has / six, and /colors).

Reading Comprehension I

▶次の文章を読み，後の問いに答えなさい。　　　　　　　　30

Ⓐ(Have you seen major leaguers eating sunflower seeds on the bench?) In many countries, people eat sunflower seeds regularly as a popular snack. In Japan, sunflower seeds are usually food for pets.

< for / what / good / sunflower / you / seeds / do / know / are >? It seems that sunflower seeds have positive effects on our health. They are filled with nutrients such as vitamin E, magnesium, and iron. Ⓑ(They are great at preventing adult disease and improving immunity.) In addition, they contain tryptophan and vitamin B6. These materials can increase the production of serotonin, which improves mental health and fights depression.

It is said that sunflowers have the ability to clean and renew polluted soil. Specifically, they may be able to remove radioactive materials from the earth.

注　　nutrient 栄養になる物　　be great at ~ ～に能力がとてもある　　prevent ～を防ぐ
　　adult disease 生活習慣病　　immunity 免疫力　　tryptophan トリプトファン
　　serotonin セロトニン　　depression うつ病　　radioactive 放射能の

1 ▶ (　)ⒶⒷをそれぞれ指定の主語から始まる付加疑問文に直しなさい。

Ⓐ　Have you seen major leaguers eating sunflower seeds on the bench?

　　→ You _____

Ⓑ　They are great at preventing adult disease and improving immunity.

　　→ They _____

2 ▶ < >内の語を「あなたはひまわりの種が何に良いか知っていますか？」という意味になるように並べ替えなさい。

< for / what / good / sunflower / you / seeds / do / know / are >?

_____

_____

3 ▶下線部を日本文に直しなさい。

It is said that sunflowers have the ability to clean and renew polluted soil.

_____

_____

Reading Comprehension II

▶次の文章を読み，後の問いに答えなさい。　　　　　　　　　　　31

　　Do you know how people ring in the New Year around the world? There are many differences between Japan and other countries.

　　Most people in English-speaking countries sing "Auld Lang Syne," a Scottish folk song, to celebrate the dawning of the New Year. This song is known as "Hotaru-no-Hikari" in Japan. It is common for Japanese to sing this song at graduation ceremonies or to hear it on New Year's Eve as a farewell song. But the original lyrics describe a situation in which old friends are enjoying a happy reunion and missing the old days with each other.

　　The Spanish eat twelve grapes to the sound of bells at midnight. This custom is meant to bring twelve happy months in the coming year.

　　In Greece, January 1st is called St. Basil's Day as well as New Year's Day. On that day the Greeks eat a traditional food called "St. Basil's cake." A coin is baked in the cake, and anyone who eats the piece of cake containing the coin will be particularly happy during the coming year.

　　Today, many countries make it a habit to set off fireworks for the celebration of the New Year.

注　　ring in ~ ～を迎える　　lyrics 歌詞　　reunion 再会

1 ▶次の質問に英語で答えなさい。

(1) For what purpose do people in English-speaking countries sing "Auld Lang Syne?"

(2) When do the Japanese sing "Hotaru-no-Hikari?"

(3) What situation do the original lyrics of "Auld Lang Syne" describe?

(4) What do the Spanish eat at midnight on New Year's Eve?

(5) What do the Greek eat on January 1st?

Chapter 11　受動態

Grammar Check　🔊 32

1 ▶ S＋V＋O の文

1) Everybody **respects** Tom. → Tom **is respected by** everybody.
2) He **washed** the car. → The car **was washed by** him.
3) They **speak** English in America. → English **is spoken** (**by them**) in America.

2 ▶ S＋V＋O＋O の文

4) She **teaches us** English. → We **are taught English by** her.
   → English **is taught to us by** her.
5) He **bought her** a doll. → A doll **was bought for her by** him.
   ※動詞が buy や make などの場合は，ふつう間接目的語を主語にした受動態にはしない。
6) I **asked him** a trivial question. → He **was asked** a trivial question **by** me.
   → A trivial question **was asked of him by** me.

3 ▶ S＋V＋O＋C の文

7) They **elected** him **mayor**. → He **was elected mayor** (by them).
8) I **found** the book **interesting**. → The book **was found interesting by** me.
9) We **call** the dog **"Shiro."** → The dog **is called "Shiro"** (by us).
   ※補語(C)は，受動態の主語にはなれない。

4 ▶ by 以外の前置詞を使う受動態

10) Everybody here **knows** him. → He **is known to** everybody here.
11) The sight **surprised** her. → She **was surprised at** the sight.
12) The news **pleased** us. → We **were pleased with** the news.
    ※驚く，喜ぶなどの感情を表す場合，英語では受動態を用いるが，日本語では「～される」と訳さない方がより自然である。

5 ▶ 助動詞のある文

13) I **must do** the work today. → The work **must be done** (by me) today.
14) We **can see** that mountain. → That mountain **can be seen** (by us).
15) You **should study** English harder. → English **should be studied** harder (by you).

6 ▶ 受動態の否定文と疑問文

16) They **don't sell** books at the store. → Books **aren't sold** at the store.
17) **Do** they **sell** books at the store? → **Are** books **sold** at the store?
18) She **didn't invite** me to the party. → I **wasn't invited** to the party by her.
19) **Did** she **invite** him to the party? → **Was** he **invited** to the party by her?
20) **Nobody thanked** me. → I **was not thanked by anybody**.

Exercises

A ▶ 次の英文を受動態の文に直しなさい。

1. Everybody loves his mother. → _____
2. She read the book. → _____
3. He taught them Chinese. → _____
4. She cooked me some sausages. → _____
5. We painted the door green. → _____

B ▶ 次の英文の( )内から適切な語(句)を選びなさい。

1. I was driven to school by (he / his / him).
2. She is (please / pleasing / pleased) with her new dress.
3. The tree was (cut / cutting / cuts) down by John.
4. (Did / Was / Had) the top of the mountain covered with snow?
5. (Are you interested / Are you interest / Do you interest) in world history?

C ▶ 次の英文の( )内から適切な語を選びなさい。

1. Butter is made (by / into / from) milk.
2. The chair is made (of / by / from) wood.
3. Milk is made (of / into / by) cheese.
4. The desks are made (into / from / by) them.
5. The car is made (at / in / by) Japan.

D ▶ 次の日本文を( )内の語(句)を用いて受動態の英文に直しなさい。

1. この犬小屋は彼が作った。　　　　　　　(doghouse)

   _____

2. この古い車は今は使われていない。　　　(old car)

   _____

3. この歌は若い人たちによく歌われている。(often, young)

   _____

4. 彼女はそのプレゼントに満足している。　(satisfied)

   _____

5. そのバケツ(bucket)には水がいっぱい入っている。(filled)

   _____

Composition

Vocabulary ▶ 語頭文字と文字数をヒントに綴りなさい。

01. 法律上の	l-(5)	02. 課する	c-(6)	03. 装置	d-(6)	04. 減らす	r-(6)
05. 肥沃な	f-(7)	06. 建築	a-(12)	07. 乱暴な	v-(7)	08. 鮮やかな	v-(5)
09. 潜在的な	p-(9)	10. 部門	d-(10)	11. 登録	r-(8)	12. 会議	c-(10)
13. ありそうな	p-(8)	14. 区別	d-(11)	15. 油断のない	a-(5)	16. 経歴	c-(6)
17. 利用できる	a-(9)	18. 法人	c-(11)	19. 深い	p-(8)	20. 調和	h-(7)
21. 強力な	p-(8)	22. 最大限	m-(7)	23. 特権	p-(9)	24. (米)国会	C-(8)
25. 実際的な	p-(9)	26. 部分	p-(7)	27. 威信	p-(8)	28. 面会, 任命	a-(11)
29. 重役	e-(9)	30. 割合	p-(10)	31. (身体が)弱い	f-(6)	32. 強烈な	i-(7)
33. 利益になる	p-(10)	34. 構造	s-(9)	35. 合理的な	r-(8)	36. 慎重な	p-(7)
37. 責任のある	r-(11)	38. (生物学上の)種	s-(7)	39. 福祉	w-(7)	40. 暇	l-(7)

Rearranging ▶ 次の日本文に合うように( )内の語に **1語を加えて**並べ替えなさい。

01. 彼女は私に毎日3度の食事を作ってくれる。　(cooked / a day / are / for / meals / me / by / three).

02. あの机は誰によって壊されましたか。　(by / broken / that / was / desk)?

03. この辺りの店は7時に閉められる。　(here / around / at / the / seven / are / stores).

04. 彼が楽しそうに歌うのが聞こえた。　(merrily / heard / he / to / was).

05. 昨日, 外国人に話しかけられた。　(I / yesterday / spoken / foreigner / by / was / a).

06. その店は午前9時に開いて, 午後6時まで開いている。
　　　　　　(the store / it / is / is / at / opened / open / 9 a.m. / 6 p.m. / , and).

07. 真相が多くの人にわかってきた。　(the / many / became / truth / people / known).

08. 彼の同僚たちは彼のことをほめる。　　　(he / his / of / by / spoken / colleagues / is).

09. 彼の家は今建築中だ。　　　　　　　　(his / now / being / house / built).

Basic Composition ▶ (　)内の条件をヒントに英文に直しなさい。

01. アメリカは Columbus によって発見された。　(5語で)

02. 私は太郎からこの本をもらった。　　　(given を用いて7語で)

03. 私たちはその犬にシュンと名づけた。　(named を用いて7語で)

04. この小説は Hemingway の作ではない。　(novel, was を用いて7語で)

05. カナダでは英語とフランス語が話されている。　(are, in を用いて7語で)

06. その会合は来週開かれる。　　　　　　(will, held を用いて7語で)

07. その猫は彼女に世話されるだろう。　　(be, care を用いて9語で)

08. そのケーキはすでに彼女に食べられてしまった。　(has, her を用いて8語で)

Applied Composition ▶ 次の日本文に合うように，下の語(句)を並べ替えて正しい英文に直しなさい。

合衆国は，多様な多民族社会で，様々な文化が存在し，たくさんの言語が話されている。人口の多様化が徐々に進んでいるので，様々なグループが一つの文化に同化しなければという強制力も弱まり，人種のるつぼとしてアメリカを語る人もだんだん少なくなってきている。今では，アメリカは多元社会であるがゆえに，サラダボウルと呼ばれている。

(a diverse, / the United States / is / nation / multiracial / in which / exist / various / cultures / and / many / are spoken / languages). (with / the diversity / a gradual / increase / in / the population, / of / there is / various / less pressure / into / a single / on / groups / to assimilate / culture, / and fewer / people / and fewer / are talking / America / about / as / a melting pot). (American / generally said / society / pluralistic / is now / to be / and it / is therefore / a salad bowl / referred to / as).

Reading Comprehension I

▶次の文章を読み，後の問いに答えなさい。　　　　　　　　　33

　　Noh is the oldest form of Japanese drama. It has been performed since the 14th century, but the origin of Noh can trace its history back to the Nara period. It consists of some characters, a flute, three kinds of drums (kotsuzumi, otsuzumi, and taiko) and a chorus. The main character is called the *shite* and the secondary character is named the *waki*.

　　Kannami (1333-1384) and his son Zeami (1363-1443) transformed Noh into the way it is performed today. The themes of almost all Noh dramas are taken from well-known Japanese works of literature such as *The Tale of the Heike*, *The Tale of Genji* and *The Tale of Ise*.

　　During the Sengoku period, Oda Nobunaga, Toyotomi Hideyoshi and Tokugawa Ieyasu were known to be eager lovers of Noh. Nobunaga and Hideyoshi even delighted in performing in Noh dramas themselves. ⒶVerification(Hideyoshi and Ieyasu protected some schools of Noh.)

注　consist of ~　〜から成る　　*shite* シテ　　*waki* ワキ
　　transform ~ into ...　〜を…に変える　　school 流派

1 ▶次の質問に英語で答えなさい。

(1) How long has Noh been performed?

(2) Who transformed Noh into the present form?

(3) What did Hideyoshi and Ieyasu protect?

2 ▶(　)Ⓐの英文を受動態の文に直しなさい。

Hideyoshi and Ieyasu protected some schools of Noh.

→

Reading Comprehension II

▶次の文章を読み，後の問いに答えなさい。　　　　　　　　　　34

The Oriental stork (kounotori) is listed as a national treasure of Japan. It is said that people saw many Oriental storks all over Japan 150 years ago, but the number of Oriental storks has decreased rapidly since then. It isn't precisely known why the number of Oriental storks dropped so sharply, but the reduction may have been caused by overhunting and Japan's rapid urbanization. For that reason, the bird has been artificially bred since the 1980's and because of this, there has been a gradual increase in the number of Oriental storks. From the standpoint of biodiversity, we must preserve the earth's environment including those wetlands on the Ramsar List.

The Oriental stork is remarkably similar to the crane. In fact, there is the view that "The Crane Lady," a famous folk story in Japan, is not about the crane but is actually about the Oriental stork. There is some evidence to support this view. Some say the stork's courtship behavior is known as "cluttering," which is a display of beak clicking. That sound, "*kata kata*," resembles that of a weaving machine. Others say many artists drew the pictures of cranes in the Edo period, but they often confused the Oriental stork with the crane. Whether "The Oriental Stork Lady" is true or not, both of them might have been familiar birds for the people in those days.

注　　national treasure of Japan 日本の天然記念物　　artificially 人工的に
　　　biodiversity 生物多様性　　Ramsar list ラムサール条約リスト
　　　beak clicking くちばしでカタカタ音を立てること

1 ▶次の質問に英語で答えなさい。

(1) Why may the number of Oriental storks have dropped sharply?

(2) How has the bird been bred since the 1980's?

(3) What is the stork's courtship behavior known as?

(4) What does the sound "*kata kata*" resemble?

(5) What did many artists of the Edo period confuse the Oriental stork with?

Chapter 12　完了形

Grammar Check　　🔵 35

1 ▶ 現在完了＜ have(has)＋過去分詞＞（継続・完了・結果・経験）

　　過去の動作・状態が現在と何らかのつながりを持っていることを示す。
- 1)　Bill **has been** in Japan since last year.
- 2)　I **haven't seen** him since Monday.
- 3)　I **have known** her for five years.
    Cf. 過去のある時に始まった**動作**が現在まで**継続**している場合は，現在完了進行形を用いる。
    They **have been playing** baseball for two hours.（2時間ずっとしている）
- 4)　I **have already washed** the dishes.
- 5)　**Have** you **done** your homework **yet**?　No, **not yet**.
- 6)　Spring **has come**.
- 7)　I **have visited** Paris five times.
- 8)　**Have** you ever **been** to Mexico?
- 9)　He **has** never **climbed** Mt. Fuji.
    ＊現在完了は，常に現在に視点を置いているので，過去を示すような語句と共に用いない。
    (×) He has climbed Mt. Fuji **last year**.
    (×) **When** have you been to Italy?

2 ▶ 過去完了＜ had ＋過去分詞＞

　　過去のある時までの完了（結果）・経験・継続を表す。それぞれの用法は現在完了に準じる。
- 10)　The train **had** already **left** when I arrived at the station.（完了）
- 11)　I **had** never **met** him before that.（経験）
- 12)　We **had lived** in Kyoto until then.（継続）
- 13)　I gave him the pen that I **had bought** a week before.（大過去）

3 ▶ 未来完了＜ will [shall] ＋ have ＋過去分詞＞

　　未来のある時までの完了（結果）・経験・継続を表す。それぞれの用法は現在完了に準じる。
- 14)　He **will have finished** studying by five.（完了）
- 15)　If I go to Hawaii again, I **will have visited** it ten times.（経験）
- 16)　They **will have been** here for six years (by) next May.（継続）

Exercises

A ▶次の英文の( )内から適切な語(句)を選びなさい。

1. I (don't / didn't / haven't) seen Tom since last week.
2. Ann (loses / lost / has lost) her bag three days ago.
3. I have (knew / known / knowing) Janet for ten years.
4. Mother (goes / gone / has gone) shopping. She isn't at home now.
5. They (sell / have sold / will have sold) all the furniture by next month.
6. I knew her at once, for I (saw / have seen / had seen) her before.

B ▶次の日本文に合うように( )に適切な語を書き入れなさい。

1. 今まで京都を訪れたことがありますか。
   Have you (　　　　　) (　　　　　　　) Kyoto?
2. 朝食をちょうど食べたところだ。
   I have (　　　　　) (　　　　　　) breakfast.
3. 吉雄はもう出発しましたか。
   Has Yoshio left (　　　　　　)?
4. どのくらいの間ここにいるのですか。
   (　　　　　) (　　　　　　) have you been here?
5. 今まで一度も北海道に行ったことがない。
   I have (　　　　　　) (　　　　　　　) to Hokkaido.
6. 彼女はフランスに行く前にフランス語を勉強したことがなかった。
   She (　　　　　) (　　　　　) (　　　　　　　) French before she went to France.
7. もし彼がもう一度霧島に行くと，そこに 10 回行ったことになる。
   If he visits Kirishima again, he (　　　　　) (　　　　　) (　　　　　　) it ten times.

C ▶次の英文に対する適切な応答文を右から選びなさい。

1. Have you read the book yet?　　　　　　(　　)　　a) For three years.
2. How long have you been in Japan?　　　(　　)　　b) Yes, I have. Twice.
3. Have you ever climbed the mountain?　(　　)　　c) No, not yet.
4. When did you come home?　　　　　　　(　　)　　d) Just an hour ago.

D ▶次の英文の下線部の誤りを訂正しなさい。

1. She showed him the pictures she <u>painted</u> in Paris.　→ _____
2. My father died after he <u>is</u> sick for a long time.　→ _____
3. Next July we <u>have married</u> for fifty years.　→ _____
4. I <u>read</u> the novel through by tomorrow.　→ _____

73

Composition

Vocabulary ▶ 語頭文字と文字数をヒントに綴りなさい。

01. 知らせる　a-(8)　02. 文学　l-(10)　03. 隠す　c-(7)　04. 熟練した　p-(10)
05. 相当する　c-(10)　06. 運ぶ　c-(6)　07. ぎょっとさせる　s-(7)　08. 流暢な　f-(6)
09. 推薦する　r-(9)　10. 演説(する)　a-(7)　11. 説得する　p-(8)　12. 破壊的な　d-(11)
13. 影響を与える　a-(6)　14. 追いかける　c-(5)　15. 心配　a-(7)　16. 定義する　d-(6)
17. に同行する　a-(9)　18. 追う　p-(6)　19. 孤立　i-(9)　20. 繁栄して　p-(10)
21. とにかく　a-(6)　22. 悲劇　t-(7)　23. 憂鬱　m-(10)　24. 割り当てる　a-(6)
25. その結果　c-(12)　26. 引き戻す　w-(8)　27. 嫌疑　s-(9)　28. 知覚する　p-(8)
29. 傍らに　a-(5)　30. 元へ戻す　r-(7)　31. 適応させる　a-(11)　32. 避けがたい　i-(10)
33. 隅から隅まで　t-(10)　34. 批評　c-(9)　35. 悪意　m-(6)　36. 熟考する　c-(11)
37. 変わることなく　i-(10)　38. 伝記　b-(9)　39. 妨げる　i-(9)　40. 終える　c-(8)

Rearranging ▶ 次の日本文に合うように( )内の語に**1語を加えて**並べ替えなさい。

01. この辺りの木の葉はすっかり落ちてしまった。　(here / all / leaves / have / around / the).

02. Tom は London を発って Edinburgh に向かった。　(has / London / Edinburgh / Tom / left).

03. 父が亡くなって10年になる。　(dead / years / father / ten / been / my / has).

04. 私は生まれたときからここに住んでいる。　(here / I / I / lived / was / have / born).

05. どこへ行ってきたのですか？公園へ行ってきたところです。　(you / have / where)? (to / the / have / I / park).

06. あなたは以前佐賀にいたことがありますか。　(been / Saga / have / before / you)?

07. 私はその前日買ったペンをなくしてしまった。
(which / I / I / the / the / bought / lost / pen / before / day).

08. 彼らはちょうど今戻ってきたところだ。　　　　　(come / just / they / back).

09. 正午までにその仕事を終えてしまっているだろう。　　(I / the / by / will / noon / finished / work).

Basic Composition ▶ (　　)内の条件をヒントに英文に直しなさい。

01. 新薬に関する報告書を書いたところだ。　　　(I, just, on を用いて10語で)

02. 彼らはまだそこに到着していない。　　　　　(6語で)

03. 彼女は先月から福岡に滞在している。　　　　(staying を用いて9語で)

04. すぐに彼女だとわかった，というのは以前に話しかけたことがあったから。
　　　　　　　　　　　　　　　　　　　　　　(recognized, at, to を用いて12語で)

05. 会合は私がそこに着いた時には始まっていた。(had, there を用いて8語で)

06. 私は彼女と知り合って5年で結婚した。　　　(had, for, we を用いて10語で)

07. 彼らはちょうど今戻ってきたところだ。　　　(過去形で5語で)

08. この本を再度読めば，3度読んだことになる。(I, if, it を用いて13語で)

Applied Composition ▶ 次の日本文に合うように，下の語(句)を並べ替えて正しい英文に直しなさい。

ある日,のんきなお爺さんが木を切りに山の中に入っていきました。木を切っていると,ぽつぽつと降り出した雨が,ザーザー降りになりました。お爺さんは,大きな木のうろ(the hollow trunk)に雨宿りの場所を見つけました。お爺さんは,腰を下ろして雨が止むのを待ちました。そして間もなく,このお爺さんはぐっすりと眠り込んでしまったのです。夕暮れ時までには降り止んだのですが,お爺さんはまだ眠り続けました。まもなく夜になり,月が出てきました。

(one day / old man / a / into / the mountains / happy-go-lucky / went / to cut wood). (he / while / was chopping, / it / to sprinkle / began / rain / with / and then, / very hard / suddenly, to rain). (the old / in the / man / found / hollow trunk / a big tree / shelter / of). (he / to wait / sat down / the rain / for / to stop, / and / asleep / fell / before long / he / fast). (it / by / early evening / raining, / had stopped / the old man / on / but / still slept). (was / soon it / nighttime, / and / came / the moon /out).

Reading Comprehension I

▶次の文章を読み，後の問いに答えなさい。　　　　　　　　　　36

Mt. Fuji, 3,776 meters high, lies in both Yamanashi and Shizuoka Prefectures. ①Since early times, the majestic mountain has been the center of Japan's mountain worship. Ⓐ< Mt. Fuji / sacred / the / considered / Japanese / have / a / symbol >. We can enjoy the beautiful sight of Mt. Fuji even from a plane or a train.
　②Mt. Fuji has had cultural significance and has often provided a motif to artists and authors. Hokusai Katsushika (1760-1849) is probably the most famous artist in the world that has painted pictures of Mt. Fuji. His work called *Thirty-six Views of Mount Fuji* is a series of pictures of Mt. Fuji in the four seasons from a wide variety of different places. Ⓑ< pictures / painted / before / of / he / he / had / 150 / Mt. Fuji / died / as many as >.
　Now many people climb Mt. Fuji to view the sunrise from the top, called "goraiko." In 2013, Mt. Fuji was declared a World Heritage site, because it has been an "object of worship" and a "source of artistic inspiration" over the ages thanks to its sacred and grand spectacle.

注　sacred 神聖な　*Thirty-six Views of Mount Fuji* 富嶽三十六景
　　be declared a World Heritage site 世界遺産に認定される

1 ▶下線部①②を日本文に直しなさい。

① Since early times, the majestic mountain has been the center of Japan's mountain worship.

② Mt. Fuji has had cultural significance and has often provided a motif to artists and authors.

2 ▶< >ⒶⒷ内の語(句)を日本文に合うように並べ替えなさい。

Ⓐ 「日本人は富士山を神聖なシンボルと考えている」
< Mt. Fuji / sacred / the / considered / Japanese / have / a / symbol >.

Ⓑ 「彼は生前に，富士山の絵を150作も描いていた」
< pictures / painted / before / of / he / he / had / 150 / Mt. Fuji / died / as many as >.

Reading Comprehension II

▶次の文章を読み，後の問いに答えなさい。　　　　　　　　　　37

　Methods of artificial weather modification have been researched for a long time. They may help people who suffer from droughts, floods and hurricanes (typhoons), but on the other hand, they may bring the danger of a weather-based weapon.

　People have attempted to control the weather through magical or religious means since early times. People have prayed for rain and fine weather in Japan as well. In the modern age, many countries have been performing a variety of experiments on weather. The most common technique of weather control is cloud seeding. It can increase rain or snow in local areas. Airplanes or cannons spray dry ice or silver iodide on clouds, as both of them cool the clouds and cause rain.

　People have also been looking for a way to avoid or to weaken hurricanes. Hurricanes feed on warm moisture and grow gradually, so the cold is their greatest enemy. In the same way as cloud seeding, airplanes approach the hurricane and seed the storm's eye with dry ice or silver iodide. Another way to weaken hurricanes is to change the air temperature. Will the day ever come when people don't suffer from bad weather?

注　artificial 人工の　weather modification 天気操作　silver iodide ヨウ化銀

1 ▶次の質問に英語で答えなさい。

(1) How have people attempted to control the weather since early times?

(2) What is the most common technique of weather control?

(3) What can cool the clouds?

(4) How do hurricanes grow?

(5) What area do airplanes seed with dry ice or silver iodide?

Chapter 13　接続詞 (II) (時制の一致を含む)

Grammar Check　🔵 38

1 ▶ 等位接続詞（See Ch. 5）
　　1)　It is late, **so** you had better go home soon.
　　2)　It may rain soon, **for** it is getting cloudy.

2 ▶「時」,「条件」を表す従属接続詞（See Ch. 5）
　　3)　**As soon as** he came home, his mother went out.
　　4)　I usually jog a few miles **before** I have breakfast.
　　5)　You must not come in **unless** I tell you to.

3 ▶「譲歩」,「原因・理由」などを表す従属接続詞（See Ch. 5）
　　6)　**Though** she is very tired, she has something to do tonight.
　　7)　**Since** I didn't know the answer, I kept silent.
　　8)　I'm glad **that** he won first prize at the exhibition.

4 ▶ 名詞節を導く従属接続詞
　　9)　It is certain **that** Dick was there at that time.
　　10)　The news **that** he is alive makes us happy.
　　11)　The fact is **that** I don't like vegetables.
　　12)　I don't know **whether** he will go to Britain (**or not**).

5 ▶ その他の従属接続詞
　　13)　He is so tall **that** he can touch the ceiling.
　　14)　Get up **as** early **as you can**.
　　15)　Do **as** you like.
　　16)　I am taller **than** Alice is.

6 ▶ 時制の一致
　　17)　She **says** that she **is** happy.　→ She **said** that she **was** happy.
　　18)　I **believe** that they **are** honest.　→ I **believed** that they **were** honest.
　　19)　I **think** that she **was** ill.　→ I **thought** that she **had been** ill.
　　20)　It **seems** that he **sold** the house.　→ It **seemed** that he **had sold** the house.

　　※時制の一致の例外（不変の真理，現在の習慣など）
　　21)　The teacher **says** that the earth **moves** around the sun.（不変の真理）
　　　　→ The teacher **said** that the earth **moves** around the sun.
　　22)　She **says** that she **goes** to bed at ten every night.（現在の習慣）
　　　　→ She **said** that she **goes** to bed at ten every night.
　　23)　He **teaches** us that Columbus **discovered** America.（歴史上の事実）
　　　　→ He **taught** us that Columbus **discovered** America.
　　24)　I **wish** I **had** a yacht.（仮定法）　→ I **wished** I **had** a yacht.

Exercises

A ▶ 次の英文の( )内に下の語群から適切な語を選び書き入れなさい。

1. She was poor, (　　　　　) she was happy.
2. Let's go home (　　　　　) it gets dark.
3. It is morning, (　　　　　) the roosters are crowing.
4. I am sorry (　　　　　) I cannot help you.

| but | though | before | for | that |

B ▶ 次の各組の英文が同じ意味になるように( )内に適切な語を書き入れなさい。

1. He is very old, but he works hard. = (　　　　　) he is very old, he works hard.
2. Run, and you'll catch the bus. = (　　　　　) you run, you'll catch the bus.
3. She was so busy that she couldn't attend the meeting.
   = She was (　　　　　) busy (　　　　　) attend the meeting.

C ▶ 次の日本文を( )内の語(句)を用いて英文に直しなさい。

1. 彼はその前の週から病気であったようだった。　(seemed, been, previous)

2. できるだけ早くここへ来てください。　(soon, can)

3. 遅い時間だが，私たちはもう少しいる。　(though, a little)

4. 彼は病気ではないかと心配だ。　(afraid, may)

D ▶ 次の英文の下線部を過去時制にして書き換えなさい。

1. He <u>doesn't know</u> that the Civil War broke out in 1861.

2. She <u>thinks</u> that the earth moves round the sun.

E ▶ 次の英文の誤りを訂正しなさい。

1. The boy didn't know that Cuba was an island country.
　_____ → _____
2. My little daughter answered that four and three were seven.
　_____ → _____
3. The other day he told me that he has seen me three years ago.
　_____ → _____
　_____ → _____
4. The teacher asked me why was I late for school.
　_____ → _____

Composition

Vocabulary ▶ 語頭文字と文字数をヒントに綴りなさい。

01. 生き残る   s-(7)
02. 化学   c-(9)
03. 哲学   p-(10)
04. おおよそ   a-(11)
05. 富ませる   e-(6)
06. 天文学   a-(9)
07. 仮説   h-(10)
08. 適当な   a-(11)
09. 差し控える w-(8)
10. 心理学   p-(10)
11. ためらう   h-(8)
12. 状況   c-(12)
13. 始め(ま)る c-(8)
14. 実証する   d-(11)
15. 救済する   r-(7)
16. 流れ   c-(7)
17. 繁栄する   t-(6)
18. 当惑させる e-(9)
19. 飢える   s-(6)
20. 明確な   d-(8)
21. 熟した   m-(6)
22. 閉じ込める c-(7)
23. 分析   a-(8)
24. 有能な   e-(9)
25. はっきりした d-(8)
26. 維持する   p-(8)
27. 謝罪   a-(7)
28. 忘却   o-(8)
29. 大気   a-(10)
30. 耕作する   c-(9)
31. 洞察(力)   i-(7)
32. 優れた   s-(8)
33. 遺伝   h-(8)
34. 熟考する   s-(9)
35. 不可欠な   i-(13)
36. かなりの   c-(12)
37. 資源   r-(8)
38. 引き受ける u-(9)
39. 気質   t-(6)
40. 関連がある r-(8)

Rearranging ▶ 次の日本文に合うように( )内の語に **1語を加えて**並べ替えなさい。

01. 暗くなったので，私たちは家路を急いだ。 (home / it / we / dark, / so / got).

02. 昨日私は家にいた，というのは雪が降っていたからだ。
(yesterday, / I / it / stayed / was / home / snowing / at).

03. 彼に今日は暇かどうか尋ねなさい。 (free / ask / is / today / he / him).

04. 雨が止むまでここで待ちましょうか。 (wait / rain / shall / stops / here / we / the)?

05. 天候不良のため試合は中止になった。
(the / the / called / bad / was / was / weather / off / game).

06. 子供の頃は貧しかったが幸せだった。 (I / I / my / was / was / though / poor / in / happy).

07. 第二次世界大戦は1945年に終わったと習った。　　(1945 / learned / we / in / World / II / War / that).

Basic Composition ▶ (　)内の条件をヒントに英文に直しなさい。

01. 私は彼が忙しいと思った。　　　　　　　　　　(that を用いて6語で)

02. Dick はそのホテルに泊まっていると言った。　　(that を用いて9語で)

03. 彼らは地球は丸いと信じていた。　　　　　　　(that を用いて7語で)

04. Mike は彼女が買い物に行ってしまったと思った。(that を用いて7語で)

05. Andrew は犯人ではないと思う。　　　　　　　(opinion, criminal を用いて9語で)

06. 彼女は知識だけでなく経験もある。　　　　　　(not, but, has を用いて8語で)

07. 彼が来るかどうかは確かではない。　　　　　　(whether, certain を用いて7語か9語で)

08. 彼は時は金なりという信念に基づいて行動する。(under, conviction を用いて9語で)

09. 鳥であればいいのになあ，と彼は言った。　　　(that, wished を用いて9語で)

Applied Composition ▶ 次の日本文に合うように，下の語(句)を並べ替えて正しい英文に直しなさい。

凶暴な鬼どもがほとんど毎晩その村を襲撃していました。鬼どもは村人たちから物を略奪したり，誘拐したり，家々を打ち壊したりしました。そこで村人たちは鬼どもを恐れていました。桃太郎 (Momotaro, the Peach boy) は，このことを聞くと，大変立腹し，鬼たちが住む鬼が島 (Demon's Island) に退治に行くことを決心しました。

(ferocious / had been / demons / raiding / every night / the village / almost). (they / the villagers / robbed / of things, / them, / kidnapped / and / houses / knocked down). (were / so / of them / the villagers / terrified). (when / Momotaro, / heard this, / the Peach Boy, / he / so angry / got / that / he / decided / that / go to / he would / Demon's Island, / demons / where / lived).

Reading Comprehension I

▶次の文章を読み，後の問いに答えなさい。　　　　　　　　　　39

Education is central to cultural, mental, and physical developments, and it can remarkably improve people's lives. ①(　　　) people need an education to support themselves, many developing countries have difficulties making kids go to school.

More than 65 million primary school-aged children aren't in school. **< to help / survive / since / can't / poor / school / usually / children / go / need / their families / to work / they / to >.** Some children give up going to school due to an ethnic conflict. It seems that as many as 800 million adults in the world are unable to read or write. People who belong to various aid institutions or projects stress the importance of education in tackling poverty. ②(　　　) parents let their children go to school, everyone will have to prevail on parents to change their minds.

注　physical 物質的　developing countries 発展途上国　ethnic conflict 民族紛争
　　institution 機関　prevail on ... to do ～するよう…を説き伏せる

1 ▶下線部①②の(　)内に適切な従属接続詞を書き入れて，日本文に直しなさい。

① (　　　　　　) people need an education to support themselves, many developing countries have difficulties making kids go to school.

_____

_____

② (　　　　　　) parents let their children go to school, everyone will have to prevail on parents to change their minds.

_____

_____

2 ▶< >内の語(句)を「**貧しい子どもたちは家族が生きるのを助けるために働く必要があるので，たいてい学校に行けない**」という意味になるように並べ替えなさい。

< to help / survive / since / can't / poor / school / usually / children / go / need / their families / to work / they / to >.

_____

_____

Reading Comprehension II

▶次の文章を読み，後の問いに答えなさい。　　　　　　　　　　　　　　　　　40

> Arthur Conan Doyle is a Scottish writer who created the series of detective fiction novels of Sherlock Holmes, such as *The Adventures of Sherlock Holmes* (1892) and *The Return of Sherlock Holmes* (1905). He published a total of 60 stories of Sherlock Holmes between 1887 and 1927. Arthur Conan Doyle, along with American writer Edgar Allen Poe, is considered "the founder of detective stories." A Japanese mystery writer used the pen name Edogawa Rampo (1894-1965), for he respected Edgar Allen Poe deeply. In *Detective Conan*, a famous Japanese cartoon, a main character named Conan Edogawa appears. His name is a mixture of the names Arthur Conan Doyle and Edogawa Rampo.
>
> Sherlock Holmes, a great detective, lives in London with his close friend Dr. Watson. Dr. Watson plays an important role as the detective's right-hand man and the narrator of the stories. Holmes says that Dr. Watson is his biographer. Holmes is cool-headed, sharp-eyed, and aggressive in his behavior. He can play the violin and has excellent boxing skills. Most importantly, he has a great knowledge of every cruel crime committed in the century and of British law. Holmes and Dr. Watson solve one mystery after another in Britain. As their reputation grows, they are invited to solve some foreign cases.
>
> The *Sherlock Holmes* series has frequently been made into movies and TV dramas. This series has attracted fans from all over the world for ages.

注　　detective 探偵　　cartoon 漫画・アニメ

1 ▶次の質問に英語で答えなさい。

(1) Who created the detective fiction novels of Sherlock Holmes?
　
(2) Why did a Japanese writer use the pen name Edogawa Rampo?
　
(3) What is Sherlock Holmes like?
　
(4) Can he play the piano?
　
(5) Why are they invited to solve some foreign cases?

Chapter 14　仮定法

Grammar Check　🔵 41

1 ▶ 仮定法過去…現在の事実に反対の仮定・想像を表す

　　If ＋主語＋(助)動詞の過去形 ; were/was …，主語＋{would, should, could, might}＋原形～

- 1) **If** I **knew** her telephone number, I **would** call her.
  ＝ As I don't know her telephone number, I won't call her.
- 2)-1 **If** my father **were** alive, he **could** see his grandson.
  ＝ As my father is not alive, he cannot see his grandson.
- 2)-2 **Were I** a bird, I **would** fly to you soon.
  ＝ **If I were** a bird, I **would** fly to you soon.

2 ▶ 仮定法過去完了…過去の事実に反対の仮定・想像を表す

　　If ＋主語＋ had ＋過去分詞 …，主語＋{would, should, could, might}＋ have ＋過去分詞～

- 3) **If** he **had worked** hard, he **would have passed** the exam.
  ＝ As he didn't work hard, he didn't pass the exam.
- 4)-1 **If** it **had** not **been** snowing heavily, I **could have gone** out.
  ＝ As it was snowing heavily, I couldn't go out.
- 4)-2 **Had he seen** you, he would have been happy.
  ＝ **If he had seen** you, he would have been happy.

3 ▶ その他の仮定法

- 5) **If** it **should** rain on the way, we will turn back.「万一…したら，～」
  ＜ If ＋主語＋ should…，主語＋助動詞(過去形あるいは現在形)～. ＞
- 6) I **wish** (＝ **If only**) I **could** fly. ＝ I am sorry I cannot fly.
  ＜ I wish ＋ S ＋仮定法過去～. ＞「～であればよいのに」(現在の願望を表す)
- 7) I **wish** (＝ **If only**) I **had seen** the film. ＝ I am sorry I didn't see the film.
  ＜ I wish ＋ S ＋仮定法過去完了～. ＞「～であればよかったのに」(過去の願望を表す)
- 8) He speaks English **as if** he **were** a native speaker.「まるで ～ であるかのように」
  ＜主節＋ as if ＋ S ＋仮定法過去～. ＞(主節の動詞の時と同時の事柄についての様態を表す)
  Cf. He looks pale **as if** he **had seen** a ghost.
- 9) **It is time** you **went** to bed.
  ＜ It is time ＋ S ＋仮定法過去～. ＞「もう～すべき(してもよい)時間だ」
- 10) **If it were not for** you, we **couldn't** carry out our plan.「もし君がいなければ，～」
  ＝ **But for** you, we **couldn't** carry out our plan.
  ＝ **Without** you, we **couldn't** carry out our plan.
  Cf. **If it had not been for** you, we **couldn't have carried** out our plan.

Exercises

A ▶ 次の英文の( )内から適切な語(句)を選びなさい。

1. He will help you if he (has / had / had had) time.
2. If my father (is / are / were) alive, I could go to college.
3. If I (have / had / had had) the money, I could have bought it.
4. If you did your best, you (could pass / had passed / could have passed) it.

B ▶ 次の英文を仮定法の文に直しなさい。

1. As the girl is weak, she can't walk all the way with us.

2. He is so old that he can't run as fast as you.

3. He did not work hard, so he failed (in) the examination.

4. As it was rainy yesterday, we could not go on a picnic.

C ▶ 次の各組の英文が同じ意味になるように( )内に適切な語を書き入れなさい。

1. As I am not so young as you, I cannot play football.
   If I (　　　　) as young as you, I (　　　　) play football.
2. I could not write a longer letter because I didn't have time.
   I could (　　　　) (　　　　) a longer letter if I (　　　　) had more time.
3. Should you change your mind, nobody would blame you.
   (　　　　) (　　　　) (　　　　) change your mind, nobody would blame you.
4. I am sorry I am not as beautiful as she.
   I (　　　　) (　　　　) (　　　　) as beautiful as she.
5. If he had seen you, he would have been happy.
   (　　　　) (　　　　) (　　　　) you, he would have been happy.

D ▶ 次の日本文を( )内の語(句)を用いて英文に直しなさい。

1. 車があれば，あなたをドライブに連れて行ってあげるのですが。　　(had, take)

2. 彼がもっと注意深ければ，同じ間違いはしないだろう。　　(careful, mistakes)

3. もしあなたが7時に家を出ていたら，7時半の電車に乗れたのに。　(the 7:30 train)

4. そろそろ学校へ行く時間よ。　　(time, went)

Composition

Vocabulary ▶ 語頭文字と文字数をヒントに綴りなさい。

01. 細菌	g-(4)	02. 妥協	c-(10)	03. 秘書	s-(9)	04. 目覚める	a-(5)
05. 主導権	i-(10)	06. 衝撃	i-(6)	07. 譲歩する	c-(7)	08. 誠実な	s-(7)
09. 探求	q-(5)	10. 取るに足らない	t-(7)	11. 断る	d-(7)	12. 反対の	c-(8)
13. 継続して起こること	s-(8)	14. 勝利	t(7)	15. 大統領	p-(9)	16. 威厳	d-(7)
17. 徴候	s-(7)	18. 刺激	s-(8)	19. 交渉する	n-(9)	20. 保守的な人	c-(12)
21. 攻撃的な	a-(10)	22. 不器用な	a-(7)	23. 最高の	s-(7)	24. 忠誠	l-(7)
25. に慣れて	a-(10)	26. 強情な	o-(9)	27. 代わりの	a-(11)	28. 良心	c-(10)
29. 不平を言う	c-(8)	30. 無限の	i-(8)	31. 服従する	s-(6)	32. 相互の	m-(6)
33. 過度の	e-(9)	34. (心の)衝動	i-(7)	35. 運動選手	a-(7)	36. 比較的な	c-(11)
37. 気が進まない	r-(9)	38. 豊富の	a-(8)	39. 外交官	d-(8)	40. 誠実	f-(5)

Rearranging ▶ 次の日本文に合うように( )内の語に **1語を加えて**並べ替えなさい。

01. 彼はまるで酔っ払っているかのように話す。　　　(he / he / were / talks / drunk / as).

02. 私に姉がいたらなあ。　　　(only / a / had / I / sister)!

03. 車の運転を習っておけばよかったなあ。　　　(I / I / drive / learned / how / had / to).

04. 彼が話すのを聞けば，あなたは彼を韓国人と間違えるだろう。
(Korean / talk, / take / would / him / him / for / you / a / hear).

05. もし太陽がなければ，何も生きられないだろう。　　　(for / sun, / live / nothing / the / could).

06. もし彼の援助がなかったら，私は失敗していただろう。
(I / help, / had / his / would / failed / been / it / not / for).

07. せめて彼に侘びくらい言ってもいいだろう。　　　　(apologize / you / least / him / to / at).

Basic Composition ▶ (　)内の条件をヒントに英文に直しなさい。

01. ギターを上手に弾くことができたらなあ。　　　　(wish を用いて 8 語で)

02. もし車を持っていれば，あなたをそこまで送っていくのですが。　(if, drive を用いて 10 語で)

03. 万一明日雨が降れば，私たちはピクニックに行きません。　(should rain を用いて 12 語で)

04. たとえ私が二百歳まで生きたとしても，その悲しい事故は決して忘れないだろう。
　　　　　　　　　　　　　　　　　　　　　　　　(were to live を用いて 18 語で)

05. もしあの時その土地を買っていたら，今頃は金持ちになっているはずだ。
　　　　　　　　　　　　　　　　　　　　　　　　(then, should を用いて 12 語で)

06. 日本人なら別の行動をとっていただろう。　　　　(differently を用いて 6 語で)

07. もしあなたが彼の立場ならどうしますか。　　　　(what, place を用いて 7 語で)

08. その薬がなかったら，私は死んでしまっただろう。　(but を用いて 8 語で)

Applied Composition ▶ 次の日本文に合うように，下の語(句)を並べ替えて正しい英文に直しなさい。

もし私たちが江戸時代に生まれていたら，私たちのほとんどは 60 歳に達することはなかっただろう。今日，医療のお陰で，私たちはかなり長生きできる。しかしながら，今日の方が昔よりも，いくつかの点で生活は危険であると言っても過言ではないだろう。例えば，毎年何千人もの人々が交通事故で亡くなったり怪我をしたりしている。

(if / born / in / had been / we / the Edo period, / very few / would / of sixty / of us / have reached / the age). (today, / we / thanks to / medical science, / can / to / a good old age / expect / to live). (exaggeration / it is, / however, / no / that / to say / today, / life / more dangerous / in / is / it was / in / some ways / than / the past). (thousands of / are killed / or injured / people, / for example, / in / every year / traffic accidents).

Reading Comprehension I

▶次の文章を読み，後の問いに答えなさい。 42

① <u>What would you do if you went to Mars?</u> NASA is planning to produce water and oxygen on the moon and Mars. A robotic car of NASA's, *Curiosity*, discovered evidence of a possible watery past on Mars.
② <u>If we want to live on Mars, we have to get vital water and oxygen.</u> ③ <u>Without water and oxygen, nothing could live.</u> But transporting water and oxygen from the Earth to Mars is difficult if not impossible. Therefore NASA plans to take carbon dioxide from the atmosphere and change it into oxygen. NASA is working steadily on the project that may lead to people living on Mars. < Mars / if / there / you / you / the future / may / should / life / go to / in / see >.

注　　Mars 火星　　oxygen 酸素　　carbon dioxide 二酸化炭素

1 ▶下線部①～③を日本文に直しなさい。

① What would you do if you went to Mars?

② If we want to live on Mars, we have to get vital water and oxygen.

③ Without water and oxygen, nothing could live.

2 ▶< >内の語(句)を，「**将来，万一火星に行くことがあったら，あなたはそこで生命を目にするかもしれない**」という意味になるように並べ替えなさい。

< Mars / if / there / you / you / the future / may / should / life / go to / in / see >.

3 ▶次の日本文を英文に直しなさい。

もし火星に行ったら，私は花と野菜を植えるだろう。

Reading Comprehension II

▶次の文章を読み，後の問いに答えなさい。

　Chushingura (The Treasury of Loyal Retainers) is the most famous and popular loyalty-revenge story in Japan based on an actual historical event at the beginning of the 18th century. In Japan, it has been made into movies and TV dramas repeatedly for years.
　In 1701, Lord Asano of the Ako domain was often disgraced by Lord Kira and hated him. Lord Asano endured the situation for ages, until he finally attempted to kill Lord Kira in the shogun's castle. After that, he was forced to commit ritual suicide as punishment for drawing a sword in the shogun's castle. Lord Asano's retainers had their property confiscated. In other words, they dropped from their positions as samurai serving their lord, to roshi (ronin) who were lordless and wandering men. If Lord Asano had thought of his retainers, he might not have acted on his hatred for Lord Kira.
　Nevertheless, a group of 47 of Asano's former retainers swore a secret oath to avenge their lord's death by killing Kira. The retainers, led by their leader Oishi, decided to sacrifice their own lives to recover their lord's honor. To conceal his secret purpose, Oishi acted foolishly, going to parties with *geisha* girls and drinking heavily in order to distract Kira's attention. As Kira was terrified of Ako's revenge, he built up his defenses but it wasn't enough. At last, Oishi and the retainers attacked Kira's mansion and carried out their vengeance against Kira on December 14th. They accepted the punishment of death by ritual suicide. This loyalty-revenge greatly moved the people of that time.
　This story has inspired artists since the 18th century. But for this historical occurrence, we couldn't enjoy these beautiful works of art.

注　　retainer 家臣　loyalty-revenge 仇討ち　domain 藩
　　　disgrace はずかしめる　ritual suicide 切腹　confiscate ～を没収する

1 ▶次の質問に英語で答えなさい。

(1) Is Chushingura a fictional TV drama?

(2) By who was Lord Asano of Ako domain disgraced?

(3) Where did Lord Asano attempt to kill Lord Kira?

(4) Why did Oishi enjoy a geisha parties and drink every night?

(5) When did Oishi and the retainers attack Kira's mansion?

Chapter 15　関係詞

Grammar Check　　🔊 44

1 ▶関係代名詞

1) I have an uncle **who** [**that**] lives abroad.（先行詞「人」，主格）
2) I know a boy **whose** father is a pilot.（先行詞「人」，所有格）
3) He is a man **whom** [**that**] I respect very much.（先行詞「人」，目的格）
4) Look at the picture **which** [**that**] is on the wall.（先行詞「人以外」，主格）
5) The house **whose** roof [the roof **of which**] is red is hers.（先行詞「人以外」，所有格）
6) The question **which** [**that**] I asked him was not easy.（先行詞「人以外」，目的格）
7) **What** he said is true.（先行詞含まれる，主格）
8) He is not **what** he was ten years ago.「10年前の彼」（先行詞含まれる，主格）

2 ▶限定用法と継続用法

9) He has two sons **who** want to work for old people.（他にも息子がいる可能性あり）
10) He has two sons, **who** want to work for old people.（= and they）
11) He broke the window, **which** made his father angry.（= and it）

3 ▶おもに that が用いられる場合

12) 先行詞に最上級の形容詞, the only, the very, the first, all, no などがつくとき
    He is **the richest** man **that** I know.
    Mr. Yoshino is **the only** person **that** supports me here.
    This is **the very** picture **that** I have long wanted to see.（まさにその）
    The first student **that** answered the difficult question was my rival.
13) 人と人以外が同時に先行詞になっている場合
    Look at **the boy and the dog that** are playing over there.

4 ▶関係代名詞の省略

14) Tom has several people (**whom**) he has to help.（目的格）(See 1.3))
15) This is the bag (**which**) she bought yesterday.（目的格）(See 1.6))
16) There is somebody (**that**) wants to see you at the gate.（There be動詞…の構文内で）
17) This is the best book (**that**) **there is** on the subject.（直後に there be動詞が続く場合）
18) He is not the man (**that**) he was ten years ago.（be動詞の補語）

5 ▶関係副詞

19) I know the day **when** she was born.（時）
    Cf. He came home at six, **when** we were having dinner.（= and then）
20) That is the house **where** my uncle lives.（場所）
    Cf. We went to Australia, **where** we stayed for a week.（= and there）
21) Do you know the reason **why** she got angry?（理由）
22) This is **how** [the way] I did it.「このようにして」（方法）
    Cf. That is **why** she is crying.「そのようなわけで…」

Exercises

A ▶ 次の２つの英文を関係代名詞を用いて１つの文に直しなさい。ただし，下線部の語を先行詞とします。

1. Tanaka is a college student. He lives in Tokyo.

2. The man was Columbus. He discovered America.

3. The girl is my sister. You met her yesterday.

4. I have a friend. Her mother is a pianist.

5. This is the first letter. I have received it from my father.

B ▶ 次の英文の（　）内に適切な関係代名詞を書き入れなさい。

1. They are the students (　　　　　) arrived here just now.
2. The mountain (　　　　　) top is covered with snow is Mt. Fuji.
3. This is the very book (　　　　　) I have wanted to read.
4. A car ran over the old man and his dog (　　　　　) were crossing the road.
5. I will lend you this book, (　　　　　) you will find interesting.

C ▶ 次の英文を日本文に直しなさい。

1. He gave me all the books that he had.

2. He was the only boy that could answer the question.

3. Tell me the name of the horse which won the race.

4. The building which you see over there is our college.

5. I remained silent, which seemed to irritate him.

D ▶ 次の日本文を（　）内の語(句)と関係代名詞を用いて英文に直しなさい。

1. パリは誰もが訪れたいと思っている都市のひとつだ。　(a city, visit)

2. これは私が今まで読んだうちで一番面白い本だ。　(have ever)

3. 私は英語の得意な学生を何人か知っている。　(several, good at)

4. 表紙の青い本が私のものだ。　(cover を用いて８語で)

5. 彼女には娘が３人いるが，３人とも医者だ。　(has)

Composition

Vocabulary ▶ 語頭文字と文字数をヒントに綴りなさい。

01. 廃止する　a-(7)　02. 不意の　a-(6)　03. 国内の　d-(8)　04. に帰する　a-(9)

05. 強要する　c-(6)　06. 野心　a-(8)　07. 民族の　e-(6)　08. 相続する　i-(7)

09. 配置する　d-(7)　10. 同時代の　c-(12)　11. 衛生の　s-(8)　12. 方言　d-(7)

13. 支配する　d-(8)　14. 習慣的な　c-(12)　15. 権威　a-(9)　16. 予算　b-(6)

17. 調査する　i-(11)　18. 熱中　e-(10)　19. 帝国　e-(6)　20. 引き出す　d-(6)

21. 欠点　f-(5)　22. 消えた　e-(7)　23. 生命のある　a-(7)　24. 打ち勝つ　p-(7)

25. に訴える　r-(6)　26. 同時の　s-(12)　27. 制度　i-(11)　28. 甘やかす　i-(7)

29. 崩壊　c-(8)　30. 栄光　g-(5)　31. 都市の　u-(5)　32. 構成する　c-(10)

33. 打ち負かす　d-(6)　34. 偏見　p-(9)　35. 予言する　p-(7)　36. 翻訳する　t-(9)

37. 犠牲　s-(9)　38. 同情　s-(8)　39. 行政　a-(14)　40. 取っておく　r-(7)

Rearranging ▶ 次の日本文に合うように( )内の語(句)に **1語**を加えて並べ替えなさい。

01. 私には米国に住んでいる姉がいる。　(have / lives / the USA / I / sister / in / a).

02. あなたの着ている服は汚れている。　(the / on / dirty / clothes / have / are / you).

03. 屋根の見える家は私の叔母のです。　(roof / house / see / aunt's / you / is / my / the / can).

04. 人間は火を使うことができる唯一の動物である。
(only / can / man / use / is / fire / the / animal).

05. ここは私が子供の頃住んでいた家だ。　(this / childhood / is / lived / the / my / I / house / in / in).

06. それが私の言いたかったことだ。　(I / that / say / is / to / wanted).

07. 5月は私が生まれた月だ。　　　　　　(born / May / I / month / is / was / the).

Basic Composition ▶ (　　)内の条件をヒントに英文に直しなさい。

01. 私はその事件について書いてある本を持っている。　(tells, case を用いて9語で)

02. あなたが会ったその男性は有名な歌手だ。　(関係代名詞を用いて9語で)

03. 彼には俊という名の息子がいる。　(関係代名詞を用いて8語で)

04. あなたの興味を引く本をすべて持っていってよい。　(interest を用いて9語で)

05. 彼はいわゆる叩き上げの男だ。　(we, self-made を用いて8語で)

06. ここは Alice と初めて会った公園だ。　(where を用いて9語で)

07. 私が黙っていると彼は怒った。　(remained, which を用いて7語で)

08. 私はこのようにして英語を学んだ。　(how を用いて6語で)

09. 私は英国に行って，そこで一ヵ月滞在した。　(where を用いて10語で)

Applied Composition ▶ 次の日本文に合うように，下の語(句)を並べ替えて正しい英文に直しなさい。

オーストラリアでは，クリスマスは夏にやってくる。一年の最も暑い時期に，グリーンクリスマスを楽しむのだ。でも，オーストラリア人は他とほぼ同じクリスマスを祝う。冬の歌であるジングルベルが街中に流れ，人工の雪がかかったクリスマスツリーがいたる所に見られる。サンタクロースもたくさんいて，顔には玉の汗を流している。

(in Australia, / arrives / in / Christmas / the summertime, / and / enjoy / people / during / a 'Green Christmas' / the year / the hottest part / of). (nevertheless, / Australians / Christmas / celebrate / in / way / much / the same / as others). (Jingle Bells, / a winter / which / is of course /song, / in / resounds / the streets, / and Christmas / covered / trees / snow / with artificial / everywhere / are seen). (plenty of / there are / also / Santas, / whose / covered / faces / with / are / sweat / beads of).

Reading Comprehension I

▶次の文章を読み，後の問いに答えなさい。　　　　　　　　　　45

① The Nobel Prize was established in 1895 under the will of Alfred Nobel (　　　) was a Swedish chemist known for the invention of dynamite. He built a vast fortune in the development and production of bombs. One day, he saw an article on his own death in a French newspaper. Ludwig Nobel, Alfred Nobel's elder brother, had died, but the press thought Alfred had died. The newspaper described Alfred Nobel as a "merchant of death," and he was strongly criticized for inventing weapons for killing people. Because he became worried about his bad reputation after his death, Alfred Nobel decided to donate his money for the creation of the Nobel Prize.

There are six categories of Nobel Prizes: physics, chemistry, physiology or medicine, literature, peace and the economics sciences. ② In 1901, the first Nobel Prize was awarded to Wilhelm Conrad Roentgen (　　　) discovered invisible light, also known as the X-ray. There have been a lot of Japanese winners of the Nobel Prize so far. <presented / usually / the Nobel Prizes / Alfred Nobel / are / when / year / every / on December 10 / died >.

注　under the will of ~ ～の遺言で　be criticized for ~ ～で批判される

1 ▶下線部①②の（　）内に適切な関係詞を書き入れて，日本文に直しなさい。

① The Nobel Prize was established in 1895 under the will of Alfred Nobel (　　　　　) was a Swedish chemist known for the invention of dynamite.

_____

_____

② In 1901, the first Nobel Prize was awarded to Wilhelm Conrad Roentgen (　　　　　) discovered invisible light, also known as the X-ray.

_____

_____

2 ▶< >内の語(句)を「ノーベル賞は通例，アルフレッド・ノーベルが亡くなった日である12月10日に毎年授与される」という意味になるように並べ替えなさい。

< presented / usually / the Nobel Prizes / Alfred Nobel / are / when / year / every / on December 10 / died >.

_____

_____

Reading Comprehension II

▶次の文章を読み，後の問いに答えなさい。　　　　　　　　　　46

　Johannes Brahms (1833-97) is usually considered one of the "Three Bs" of classical music: Bach, Beethoven, and Brahms.
　He began piano lessons as a child, and three years later he was already able to take part in a chamber musical recital. He played the piano mostly in taverns and in dance halls as his job to supplement the family income. After that, he became a collaborative pianist and went on a tour with a violinist, Eduard Remenyi. During his tour, he visited Robert Schumann (1810-1856) who was a famous critic and composer. At Schumann's home, Brahms performed several numbers that he had composed by himself and Brahms won praise from Schumann. After that, Schumann wrote an article admiring Brahms for his ability to compose great music, which greatly helped Brahms's career. But what was important was that Brahms met Clara, Schumann's wife and a pianist herself. At that time, he was 20 years old and she was 14 years older than him.
　Brahms admired the Schumanns and devoted himself completely to the Schumann family. Brahms became gradually attracted to Clara and eventually fell in love with her. Though a close relationship developed between Brahms and Clara, he was indebted to Robert Schumann. Because of this, he decided to part ways with her after Schumann's death.

注　tavern 居酒屋　collaborative pianist 協演ピアニスト
　　be indebted to ~ ~に恩義がある　part ways with ~ ~と決別する

1 ▶次の質問に英語で答えなさい。

(1) Where did Brahms originally play the piano?

(2) During his tour, who did Brahms visit?

(3) What did Brahms do at Schumann's home?

(4) How old was Clara when they first met?

(5) Why did Brahms and Clara part even after Robert Schumann's death?

著作権法上、無断複写・複製は禁じられています。

ELEMENTARY ENGLISH READING & WRITING　　[B-779]
英文法から学ぶ英作と読解

1	刷	2015年2月12日
6	刷	2023年3月31日

著　者　　佐藤　哲三　　　Tetsuzo Sato
　　　　　伊藤　真紀　　　Maki Ito
発行者　　南雲　一範　　Kazunori Nagumo
発行所　　株式会社　南雲堂
　　　　　〒162-0801　東京都新宿区山吹町361
　　　　　NAN'UN-DO Co., Ltd.
　　　　　361 Yamabuki-cho, Shinjuku-ku, Tokyo 162-0801, Japan
　　　　　振替口座：00160-0-46863
　　　　　TEL：　03-3268-2311（営業部：学校関係）
　　　　　　　　03-3268-2384（営業部：書店関係）
　　　　　　　　03-3268-2387（編集部）
　　　　　FAX：03-3269-2486
編　集　　加藤　敦
製　版　　木内　早苗
装　丁　　Nスタジオ
検　印　　省　略
コード　　ISBN 978-4-523-17779-1　C0082

Printed in Japan

E-mail　nanundo@post.email.ne.jp
URL　https://www.nanun-do.co.jp/